R

It's Jesus Calling!
Why You Should
Throw Away Your Copy of Jesus Calling

Steven Hudgik

Move to Assurance
P.O.Box 277
Cannon Beach, OR 97110

ISBN-10: **1517766869**
ISBN-13: **978-1517766863**

SOURCES OF SCRIPTURE QUOTATIONS

Unless otherwise noted, scripture is taken from the NEW AMERICAN STANDARD BIBLE, copyright © 1960, 1963, 1968, 1971, 1972, 1973, 1975, 1977, 1995 by The Lockman Foundation. Used by permission.

In a few places two other translations have been used and are indicated by the following abbreviations:

ESV: Scripture quotations are from The Holy Bible, English Standard Version® (ESV®), copyright © 2001 by Crossway, a publishing ministry of Good News Publishers. Used by permission. All rights reserved.

NKJV - Scripture taken from the New King James Version®. Copyright © 1982 by Thomas Nelson. Used by permission. All rights reserved.

DEDICATION

My deepest gratitude to SW Hills Baptist Church, and the many people from SWHBC, as well as from other churches, who have supported my ministry and the Cannon Beach Bible Church through your prayers, many volunteer hours, financial giving, and other donations. THANK YOU!!! I dedicate this book to you. Your giving has made it possible to begin the process of replanting and restarting the Cannon Beach Bible Church.
THANK YOU VERY MUCH!

Beloved, do not believe
every spirit, but test the spirits to
see whether they are from God,
for many false prophets
have gone out into the world.
1 John 4:1 (ESV)

CONTENTS

For the time is coming when
people will not endure
sound teaching, but having
itching ears they will accumulate
for themselves teachers to suit
their own passions.
2 Timothy4:3 (ESV)

THANK YOU!

My thanks to Tim, Kay, Karen, Denny and Arlene who started me down the path to investigating *Jesus Calling*. Their questions and insights led me to examine *Jesus* Calling and quickly conclude that this is a book Christians should run from.

I'd like to express my deepest thanks and appreciation to Wendi McCloy and Bob Brown for reviewing an early draft of this book. Their comments, questions and suggestions have resulted in significant improvements. They have helped make this book complete, and more cohesive and interesting to read. Thank you Wendi and Bob!

I also thank my 91 year old father, Frank Hudgik, who hosted me in his home for 2-1/2 weeks while I was on "vacation." He gave me the free time I needed to write the first draft of this book. Getting started is the hardest part, and I never would have gotten started without the gift of time my father gave me.

And thank you to my wife Eileen for putting up with me while I sat in front of the computer for endless hours. Without her steady support, her "protecting" me from interruptions, and her gracious patience, as well as the continuous supply of food she prepared, writing this book would have been difficult.

And above all, Lord Jesus Christ thank you! Father thank you! Holy Spirit thank you! You have at times guided me, and you have at times protected me, you have given me the strength, and you have used some unique ways to keep me in front of the computer getting this book completed. THANK YOU above all else and above all others!

ALL PRAISE TO GOD!!

Beware of false prophets,
who come to
you in sheep's clothing
but inwardly
are ravenous wolves.
Matthew 7:15 (ESV)

INTRODUCTION

Beloved, do not believe every spirit, but test the spirits to see whether they are from God, because many false prophets have gone out into the world.
- 1 John 4:1

Beware of false prophets, who come to you in sheep's clothing but inwardly are ravenous wolves. — Matthew 7:15 (ESV)

Now these were more noble-minded than those in Thessalonica, for they received the word with great eagerness, examining the Scriptures daily to see whether these things were so. — Acts 17:11

Several years ago a woman came to me and asked about a book called *Jesus Calling®*. I am the head of an apologetics and evangelism ministry and I get a lot of questions. But, I had never heard of this book. So, I borrowed her copy and started reading random devotions. I hadn't read very many before I was repulsed by what I was reading. This book was written as though Jesus was speaking everything in the book, and this was not the Jesus I knew from scripture!

Since then I've lost count of the number of people who have asked me about *Jesus Calling*. I've reached the point at which, instead of covering the same ground over and over, I thought it best to write it down and create a book I could just hand to people. This is that book.

What is *Jesus Calling?*

Jesus Calling is a devotional book written by Sarah Young that was first published in 2004. I'll let the publisher describe this book:

> *"Sarah Young's devotional writings are personal reflections from her daily quiet time of Bible reading, praying, and writing in prayer journals. With sales of more than 14 million books worldwide, Jesus Calling® has appeared on all major bestseller lists. Sarah's writings include Jesus Calling®, Jesus Today?® Jesus Lives™, Dear Jesus, Jesus Calling® for Little Ones, Jesus Calling® Bible Storybook, Jesus Calling®: 365 Devotions for Kids, and Peace in His Presence—each encouraging readers in their journey toward intimacy with Christ. Sarah and her husband were missionaries in Japan and Australia for many years. They currently live in the United States."* - On line Promotional blurb by the publisher of Jesus Calling, Thomas Nelson (http://tiny.cc/hitz4x)

Many of you may be familiar with *Jesus Calling*, and a large number of you have probably read at least part of it. However, for those of you who have never heard of *Jesus Calling*, this introduction is for you. It provides a short overview of the *Jesus Calling* devotional.

As you start reading *Jesus Calling* you'll immediately notice that the devotions are written in the first person, with Jesus speaking. Here is a random example – January 10th:

> *"EVERY TIME YOU AFFIRM YOUR TRUST IN ME, you put a coin into My treasury."* - Jesus Calling, January 10th, The 10th Anniversary Edition, page 11 (capitalization as in the original).

Who is "ME in the above quote?" That's Jesus speaking. *Jesus Calling* is written as though Jesus is speaking directly to you. This makes it a very different type of devotional book and, as you'll learn by reading this book, it also results in quite a few problems.

A second characteristic of *Jesus Calling* is that it uses Christian words and language in a way that makes it sound very Christian. But, in many cases what it says is so vague that the reader can easily read into it whatever they happen to be thinking. And when there is a discernable meaning, it frequently is not in accordance with what scripture teaches. The result is vague and unbiblical teaching coming from the lips of Jesus, but it is worded such that on the surface it appears to be good Christian teaching.

A third characteristic of the *Jesus Calling* devotions is that they are based on "messages" the author "believes" she received from Jesus as a result of her asking Jesus to guide her thoughts. This type of experience is similar to New Age practices used to receive spiritual messages. Combine this with the devotions being spoken by "Jesus", and you have a book that has given itself a very high level of perceived authority... after all, these are words directly from "Jesus."

Add this all together and what we have in *Jesus Calling*, is a "devotional" that is unlike any other Christian devotional. Jesus is speaking to you using Christian words and phrases, but what he says is often not scriptural, or is so indefinite that the reader can make it mean whatever they already believe. Combined with the author's claims that these devotions are based on messages received from Jesus, the result is a perceived doctrinal accuracy and authority that does not exist. What readers get, instead of an author sharing her personal reflections—as is claimed in the publisher's blurb, and is normal for other devotionals—is a devotional in which "Jesus"... God... speaks directly to you, telling you how to think and what to do. *Jesus Calling* is a very dangerous book.

In a review of *Jesus Calling* Rick Thomas wrote:

> *This book is claiming to add to the written revelation we have already received in the Word of God. I know I keep emphasizing this, but it's so dangerous. No, I don't think Young is proposing to add the book of Young after Revelation. But that is, in effect, what her writings are claiming.* – Rick Thomas (http://tiny.cc/ocsz4x)

Jesus Calling has achieved a level of sales unmatched by most other devotionals. Millions of people are reading *Jesus Calling*. Millions of people are applying what they learn from *Jesus Calling* to their lives. That's a big problem.

What we will be doing in this book is examining, step-by-step, potential problems with *Jesus Calling*. Then we'll learn what the real Jesus is like by looking at what He actually says in scripture. The best way to identify a counterfeit Jesus is to know the real Jesus.

Two ways to know false teaching

There are two sure-fire ways to identify false teaching. One is that it presents a false Jesus... and we'll see that *Jesus Calling* does that. The other is that it presents a false gospel... and we'll see that *Jesus Calling* does that also. We'll also see that *Jesus Calling* is filled with unbiblical teaching.

What is the best way to identify a counterfeit Jesus?

By knowing the real Jesus and the real gospel.

RUN! It's Jesus Calling is not a negative book. Most of this book is about the real Jesus and what He actually said. If you know the real Jesus, you'll see the "Jesus" of *Jesus Calling* is shallow, superficial, and not concerned about the gospel—meaning the Jesus of *Jesus Calling* is not the loving Jesus whose reason for coming to earth was to save us. His #1 goal is that none would perish.

> *The Lord is not slow about His promise, as some count slowness, but is patient toward you, not wishing for any to perish but for all to come to repentance.* - 2 Peter 3:9

This verse does not mean everyone is saved. What Peter is saying is that Jesus loves you and does not want you to perish. That's why He came. But, although not stated in this verse, you have the option of rejecting Him and following a false Jesus. It's your choice. Please make the right choice and choose Jesus, the right Jesus. Not the Jesus of *Jesus Calling*.

I'd like to conclude with a word to some of my charismatic brothers and sisters. As you read this book you'll notice that I do not believe anyone today is receiving messages from God in the same way as claimed by Sarah Young. I have good reasons for my position, which I touch on lightly in this book. However, without regard to our differences on that subject, please at least read the prolog, and then evaluate whether *Jesus Calling* presents a true or false gospel. I think you'll agree it is a false gospel and on that point alone *Jesus Calling* must be rejected as being a book that is good for Christians to read.

PROLOGUE

For I am conscious of nothing against myself, yet I am not by this acquitted; but the one who examines me is the Lord. - 1 Corinthians 4:4

I will not acquit the guilty – Exodus 23:4

It was late on Saturday evening. This book was finished and I was a few seconds away from clicking the button that would finalize it for publication. But, I didn't click.

I was pushing hard to make my deadline, and with the help of my wife we were going to make it! After a final week of 16 hour days working on corrections, catching typos, and adding the graphics, the book was ready. It was time to celebrate!

But, I didn't click on the button.

There was something missing. And not just something minor, it might possibly be the most important part of the book. This crucial information was already in the book, but it was buried in several chapters in the middle of the book. What was needed was a chapter at the beginning, a prolog that immediately brought this needed information to light.

It's always about Jesus

In writing this book my focus has been on Jesus. I begin in chapter one by showing that the name of Jesus is being misused, and then I continue on, step-by-step, showing that the Jesus of *Jesus Calling* is not the Jesus of the bible. As we go through *Jesus Calling*, comparing it with scripture, you'll also learn what the real Jesus said. The last section of this book completely focuses on the words of the real Jesus. Presenting a false Jesus, as *Jesus Calling* does, is a sure sign of false teaching. Presenting the real Jesus is the best way to reveal the false.

Another sign of false teaching:

Another sure sign of false teaching is that it includes a false gospel. Does *Jesus Calling* present a false gospel? Yes, it does.

What I say in this prolog I've already said in other chapters in the book. I know, you haven't read them yet, but the prolog is the last section I wrote. This prolog may even save you a lot of time by highlighting two of the devotions in which a false gospel of salvation is presented. You can read the prolog; see that *Jesus Calling* is false teaching; then throw away your copy of *Jesus Calling* and move on.

Where does *Jesus Calling* present a false gospel?

When you get to Chapter 16, which talks about peace, you will find a section that plainly and simply shows that the July 3rd *Jesus Calling* devotion preaches a false gospel.

> *"I have acquitted you through My own blood. Your acquittal came at the price of My unparalleled sacrifice."* – Jesus Calling, 10th Anniversary Edition, 2014, July 3rd, page 194

What does "acquit" mean? The dictionary definition is: *to free (someone) from a criminal charge by a verdict of not guilty* (Oxford Dictionary of English). That means the court has determined that you never committed the crime. You are innocent. In the case of *Jesus Calling*, "Jesus" is saying you were acquitted, meaning you never sinned… that there never was a crime. And that's a lie. God does not lie.

> *If we say that we have no sin, we are deceiving ourselves and the truth is not in us.* – 1 John 1:8

Scripture uses words such as redeemed, atonement, and propitiation to describe what Christ's blood did. He REDEEMED us by paying the penalty that we earned. This was accomplished through His atonement, His dying as a substitute for us. And it resulted in propitiation – the wrath of God is appeased and we are reconciled to Him.

If you were acquitted, that means you are innocent… you never sinned. So there is no need for punishment, and no reason for the cross. Jesus died for nothing. There is no need for the blood of Jesus, because there is no penalty to be paid. To say you have been acquitted by the blood of Jesus is a false gospel, it is a logically meaningless statement, and it does away with the need for redemption, atonement, and propitiation.

Here's the truth of the gospel: you are guilty. You have broken God's laws. You are standing before the judge and the verdict is guilty… the penalty is death. Then Jesus steps up and says, *"I'll pay the penalty for this person."* And Jesus pays, in full, the penalty you've earned for sin. That's why scripture never uses the word "acquit" but refers to this as "redeemed." You are guilty, and have earned the just penalty for sin. But, you have been redeemed by Christ. This means Jesus paid the price to free you from the penalty for sin. You have been justified, which means that, although you are guilty, because Christ paid your penalty in full you have been declared by God to be righteous. You are free! All you need to do is trust this is true, and this free gift is yours. Pray now, confessing your sins and thanking God for His grace and mercy.

I am afraid of all my pains, I know that You will not acquit me. I am accounted wicked. – Job 9:28 & 29a

Are there any other places where *Jesus Calling* presents a false gospel?

In chapter 15 I discuss another instance of *Jesus Calling* presenting a false gospel of salvation. Let's look at a quote from the 10th Anniversary Edition of *Jesus Calling*, published in 2014.

"PEACE BE WITH YOU! Ever since the resurrection this has been My watchword to those who yearn for Me. As you sit quietly, let My Peace settle over you and enfold you in My Loving Presence. To provide this radiant Peace for you, I died a criminal's death. Receive My peace abundantly and thankfully." – February 13th, page 46.

Scripture tells us our peace comes from being reconciled to God, in other words from our salvation. Based on the above quote, what did Jesus do to provide peace for you? He died a criminal's death. Is this a true statement?

It is true that Jesus died a criminal's death. The cross was a way that criminals were executed. But, was it His dying a criminal's death that saved you? Or are you reading your Biblical knowledge into this statement?

Ted Bundy died a criminal's death, executed in the electric chair in Florida. He was a serial killer who brutally murdered 30 women. Apparently he was the same as Jesus... he died a criminal's death. No! The only time someone who dies a criminal's death saves someone else, is when the wrong person is executed.

What did Jesus actually do to provide peace for us? It wasn't because he died a criminal's death. It was because He died, taking the full wrath of God for sin onto Himself, paying the penalty we've earned as a result of our breaking God's laws. Jesus' substitutionary death on the cross is what saves us from God's wrath. Jesus redeemed us. He paid the price we owed for our sin. You won't read about that anywhere in *Jesus Calling*. Saying that we have peace because Christ died a criminal's death is a false gospel.

I've provided two witnesses... two examples showing the *Jesus Calling* presents a false gospel. There are others, such as June 14th, but even one is sufficient.

But even if we or an angel from heaven should preach to you a gospel contrary to the one we preached to you, let him be accursed. – Galatians 1:8 (ESV)

Whenever someone asks you about *Jesus Calling*, tell them to read the prolog. The rest of this book is packed with good information, but the prolog alone is sufficient to show *Jesus Calling* is not a Christian book and needs to be treated as false teaching... in other words get rid of it!

PART I – THIS IS NOT JESUS CALLING

CHAPTER 1
SINFUL OR ACCEPTABLE?

Let's just jump in and get started by looking at the most obvious potential problem: *Jesus Calling* is written as though Jesus is speaking. Is that sinful or is that acceptable to God? I'm big on being sure we're all on the same page as far as definitions, so let's start by answering the question:

What is sin?

Sin is acting or thinking in a way that is contrary to how God acts and thinks. Righteousness is the opposite of sin. Righteousness is acting and thinking in accordance with the character of God. You are sinning any time you are not being righteous. So you are sinning whenever you act or think in a way contrary to how God acts or thinks. This is because you were created in the image of God. When you do not reflect that image, you are sinning.

To help us know the character of God, He has given us His laws, such as the Ten Commandments. God's laws describe His character and what we should be like. If we break God's laws, we are sinning... we are not behaving in a way that is consistent with God's character.

So, this is the question: is writing *Jesus Calling* in a way such that "Jesus" is speaking the words of each devotion sinful or righteous? Is it acting in accordance with God's character or is it acting contrary to the character of God?

Let's take a look at the opening line of the January 16th *Jesus Calling* devotion. This is typical of all the *Jesus Calling* devotions:

> *"Come to ME, and rest in My loving Presence."* - Jesus Calling January 16th, 2004, page 17 (capitalization as in original).

You may not have a copy of *Jesus Calling* handy so you can look up the context, but the *"ME"* and *"My"* in the above quote refers to "Jesus." This is "Jesus" speaking.

Let's stop and think: Who is Jesus? He is God. When God speaks, and His words are recorded in writing, what are they called? That's an easy question, they are scripture.

Since the words in *Jesus Calling* are coming from the lips of the Son of God, then the book *"Jesus Calling"* should be added to the Bible. If we take it at face value, as it is written *Jesus Calling* is an additional revelation from God. There is no question about this, because it is God who is speaking.

If this book were fiction Jesus could be shown as speaking. I don't agree with that being acceptable to God, but at least it would be identified as fiction. But, the author of *Jesus Calling* never represents *Jesus Calling* as fiction. The *Jesus Calling* devotions are presented as factual, giving instructions, advice and commands that come from the lips of "Jesus." Putting these words in the mouth of Jesus makes them equivalent to scripture.

But, I can hear those of you who have a copy of *Jesus Calling* saying... "In the introduction to *Jesus Calling* Sarah Young states: '*I knew these writings were not inspired as Scripture is...*'" (Jesus Calling, 2004 edition, page XII).

Sarah Young plainly states in the introduction to *Jesus Calling* that what she has written is not scripture.

What does it mean to say something is not scripture? One thing it means is that it could not have been spoken by Jesus. Everything Jesus speaks is perfect, true and without error... in other words it is scripture. If it comes from the mouth of Jesus, it is scripture. If it's not scripture, then it cannot be Jesus speaking. So we have to ask, if it is not scripture, why is Jesus represented as speaking these words?

If Jesus is represented as saying something He never said, what is that called?

It is lying. And that means *Jesus Calling* is blasphemy. It is a lie to put any words in Jesus' mouth that he did not say. In later chapters we'll learn that many of the words that have been put on the lips of our Savior are not Biblical. But, that's another issue. For now we're just talking about a devotional book that is neither scripture nor fiction, in which Jesus is made out to be speaking.

That book is blasphemy. God never spoke the words the book is representing Him as saying. That means it is a lie to have these words coming from the lips of God. Christians know lying is wrong. We are to have the character of God, and lying is a major violation of God's character.

Do you think I'm being too harsh? Maybe too legalistic? When God is represented as having said something He never said, what would you call that? (Write your answer here: _____ _____.)

I'll get back this question in a later chapter.

What is blasphemy?

Blasphemy is doing or saying something that does not show proper reverence for God. Blasphemy is also doing or saying something that harms God's reputation... something that detracts from His glory. Putting words into the mouth of Jesus, words Jesus never said—Sarah Young says they are not scripture, so Jesus could never have said them—is misrepresenting God. It is attributing a lie to God. It is representing God as someone He is not... that's blasphemy.

> *"Whenever anybody places words in the mouth of God that God did not say, they are misrepresenting Him as well. To write a book and present that book to others as the words of Jesus talking to them goes way beyond the standard practice of an author writing their thoughts and beliefs. They have taken their words and exalted them to the status of equality with the Bible no matter what claim they try to make otherwise."* - Robert Alan King, A Christian Rebuttal to Sarah Young's Jesus Calling, Introduction, 2011 Kindle book

So why did Sarah Young write this book with Jesus speaking all of the devotions?

In her introduction to *Jesus Calling* Sarah Young writes:

> *"I have written from the perspective of Jesus speaking to help readers feel more personally connected with Him* [Jesus]" – Jesus Calling, 2014 10th Anniversary Edition, page XIII

In her words, the reason is so that you will feel more personally connected with Jesus. Can you become more personally connected with Jesus by reading something that misrepresents Jesus... something that has Jesus saying things He never said? No. You'd be reading a lie. Misrepresentation is a form of lying. Lying is a sin and sin doesn't bring you closer to Jesus, it separates you from Jesus.

> *But your iniquities have made a separation between you and your God, and your sins have hidden His face from you so that He does not hear.*
> – Isaiah 59:2

Sarah Young is right in one respect. You can feel more personally connected with the "Jesus" of *Jesus Calling*. But, that does not mean you are growing closer to the real Jesus, the Son of God. The reality is you are *"becoming more personally connected to"* a lie. To a "Jesus" who does not exist. And that means you are moving further away from the real Jesus and closer to a false Jesus. Even a small lie moves you away from Jesus.

Yes, even a small lie about Jesus represents the almighty creator God as being less than who He is... less than the perfect, eternal, omniscient, holy, righteous, loving God we know from scripture. Never forget Jesus IS GOD. And never forget who God is.

> For the LORD your God is God of gods and Lord of lords, the great, the mighty, and the awesome God. - Deuteronomy 10:17

Here's another question: Does the "Jesus" of *Jesus Calling* sound anything like the Jesus of the Bible? Read the book of Isaiah starting with chapter 40. This is the true Jesus speaking:

> Listen to Me, O Jacob, even Israel whom I called; I am He, I am the first, I am also the last. Surely My hand founded the earth, And My right hand spread out the heavens; besides Me there is no God. - Isaiah 48:12-13

Who is speaking here? The Son of God, Jesus. These words, as well as most of Isaiah chapters 40 through 66, are a direct quotes from Jesus. They are the words of the Son of God. How do we know that? Go to Isaiah 48:16

> Come near to Me, listen to this: From the first I have not spoken in secret, From the time it took place, I was there. **And now the Lord GOD has sent Me, and His Spirit.**

Who did the sending? "The Lord God," the Father.

Who was sent? The speaker, "Me." That can only be the Son. The One who has been speaking since the beginning of chapter 40.

Who was also sent? The Spirit.

Here in the Old Testament we see the Trinity. The Father is doing the sending. It is the Son who has been speaking since chapter 40. And the Spirit was also sent. These are the words of Jesus Christ, the Son of God. This is what the true Jesus Christ sounds like. His words have a depth and richness to them not found in *Jesus* Calling. This is not the Jesus of the *Jesus Calling* devotional book.

Never forget Jesus IS GOD. You do not become more personally

14

connected to God through words placed in His mouth by a human writer... words He never said... and as we'll see in a few chapters, words that in many cases contradict what the real Jesus has said in the Bible. Any form of a lie is sin, and sin separates us from God.

The *Jesus Calling* devotions ARE NOT the true Jesus calling.

> Many Christians today are greatly concerned about the rising influences of communism, humanism, secularism, and social injustice. Yet those evils, great as they are, do not together pose the threat to Christianity that false shepherds and pastors do. Throughout the history of redemption, the greatest threat to God's truth and God's work has been false prophets and teachers, because they propose to speak in His name. That is why the Lord's most scathing denunciations were reserved for the false teachers of Israel, who claimed to speak and act for God but were liars.
>
> -- John MacArthur, Was Jesus Polite to False Teachers?, September 27, 2013

CHAPTER 2
IS THIS REALLY JESUS SPEAKING?

"I decided to 'listen' with pen in hand, writing down whatever I 'heard' in my mind... This is how I was listening to Him—by focusing on Jesus and His word, while asking Him to guide my thoughts. I was not listening for an audible voice; I was spending time seeking God's Face." - Jesus Calling, Introduction to the 2014 Anniversary Edition, page XII

This is the source of the teaching in *Jesus Calling*, as described by the author, Sarah Young. We can get additional details from the original introduction that was included in *Jesus Calling* from 2004 until 2014:

"I decided to listen to God with pen in hand, writing whatever I believed He was saying. I felt awkward the first time I tried this, but I received a message. It was short, biblical, and appropriate. It addressed topics that were current in my life: trust, fear, and closeness to God. I responded by writing in my paper journal." - Jesus Calling, 2004 edition, page XII

To summarize, what we have is Sarah Young:

- Beginning by focusing on god and his word
- Asking god to guide her thoughts
- Seeking god's face,
- Listening to god with pen in hand, and then
- Receiving messages from god

16

- Writing down what she believed god was saying
- Writing whatever she "heard" in her mind

Notice she says that she is writing down what she "BELIEVED" God was saying, writing "whatever" she heard in her mind. When we trust the *Jesus Calling* book, who are we actually trusting? That's another easy question, we're trusting Sarah Young.

When you read and believe *Jesus Calling* you are trusting that what Sarah Young "believed" she heard was actually God communicating to her. You are trusting that a fallible person received messages from God in her fallible thoughts, and wrote them down correctly. You are trusting that all of this was done accurately and without error.

My next question is: How does she know this was really God giving her messages? We speak to ourselves in our thoughts. Demons can whisper thoughts in our ears. How can we, as fallible persons, correctly discern thoughts guided by God from our own thoughts, or the words of demons?

None of these questions and problems are addressed in the *Jesus Calling* book. You just have to trust Sarah Young. Is this where you want to put your trust? In a fallible human being?

The end result is a book written in the first person, with Jesus speaking. So you get a false assurance that you can trust what is being said because it is coming from "Jesus." But, can you trust this book?

Scripture tells us that, to know if something is of God we need to test it by comparing it with scripture. If there is any part, even a minor part that is not 100% in agreement with scripture, none of it is from God. Sarah Young gives no indication of having done this. We'll do that for *Jesus Calling* in Part II of this book. It will reveal that *Jesus Calling* is not Biblical and is not from God.

Carefully consider what Sarah Young says about how she received these messages. Based on her descriptions, she is receiving "messages" as a result of her asking God to guide her thoughts. Then she is writing what she believes God is communicating. It's a process that is totally dependent on Sarah Young's perceptions and thoughts, and as a result does not appear to be reliable.

In my opinion Sarah Young should have written the truth. *Jesus Calling* should be written in her voice describing her experiences and thoughts. Let's look at an example of what I mean using the opening line from the devotion for June 1st (2004 edition, page 169) in which Jesus says:

"I am involved in each moment of your life."

Since in *Jesus Calling* she is writing her thoughts, she should express them as her thoughts,

Jesus is making a straight-forward declarative statement. If Sarah Young was writing something more in line with how she has described receiving these message, she might have written something such as:

"After meditating on the greatness of God I began to understand that God is involved in each moment of our lives."

Since in *Jesus Calling* she is writing her thoughts, she should express them as her thoughts, not as the words of Jesus... the words of God. To write her thoughts as though Jesus were speaking them is sin... and sin separates us from God.

"It seems obvious to me that Young has projected her thoughts of what Jesus would say to her onto paper, as if it was Jesus speaking to her. If that is the case, she is making Jesus out in her own image, and the content certainly bears that out." - Cripplegate, August 22, 2012 (https://thecripplegate.com/the-jesus-calling/)

Remember, our "heart"—that's our inner being, including our thoughts—cannot be trusted. Scripture says:

18

The heart is deceitful above all things, and desperately wicked: who can know it? - Jeremiah 17:9 (KJV)

Jesus Calling is not scripture. Misrepresenting these words as coming from Jesus is blasphemy. Because of the way *Jesus Calling* is written this book misleads people to have more confidence than they should in what this book says.

Be wary, this IS NOT the TRUE Jesus calling.

The plain fact is, all that is wanted by many today is merely a soothing position for their conscience, which will enable them to go on comfortably in a course of self-pleasing, which will permit them to continue their worldly ways without the fear of eternal punishment.

— A. W. Pink, Studies In The Scriptures, July 1953, page 9

CHAPTER 3
JESUS SPEAKING MAKES
THE BOOK MORE INTERESTING

"I have written them from Jesus' point of view; i.e., the first person singular (I, Me, Mine) always refers to Christ. 'You' refers to you, the reader, so the perspective is that of Jesus speaking to you." - Sarah Young, Jesus Calling Introduction, 2004, pages XIII and XIV

Several people who have asked me about *Jesus Calling* have told me: *"It's no big deal. It's just a point of view. Having Jesus speak the words in Jesus Calling helps make the book more interesting to read."*

To say this is to forget who we are talking about... God. It is a big deal. Does God lend His name to be used in a book just so that book will be more interesting? No, never!

You cannot buy or borrow the name of God to help make a book, a movie, a theme park, or anything else more interesting. God is not some famous movie star, TV pitchman, or flim-flam man willing to have his name attached to any book or product someone wishes to sell. God is holy. Only what is of God, may be attributed to God.

Remember who God is:

As for God, His way is perfect; The word of the LORD is proven; - 2 Samuel 22:31 (NKJV)

Thus says the Lord, your Redeemer, and the one who formed you from the

womb, "I, the Lord, am the maker of all things, Stretching out the heavens by Myself and spreading out the earth all alone, Causing the omens of boasters to fail, Making fools out of diviners, Causing wise men to draw back And turning their knowledge into foolishness." – Jesus speaking in Isaiah 44:24-25

Let's think about this. What is accomplished by writing a devotional book from the point of view of Jesus (God)? It gives authority to what is said. Authority it does not deserve, since these are not actually the words of Jesus.

Without regard to what the author may have intended, many readers are left with the impression that Jesus is speaking to them personally through this devotional book. The words of Jesus have authority... Jesus is God. And for that reason, only the actual words of Jesus... the words of scripture... should ever be attributed as coming from Jesus.

Sarah Young is not just writing from any point of view, let's say the point of view of a famous pastor. She is writing from the point of view of God. No one should do that, unless they are writing the inspired word of God... in other words unless it is scripture that is being written. Otherwise, what is written is deceptive. Why? Because, coming from God's lips, it appears to have authority and trustworthiness that, in reality, it doesn't have.

While she acknowledges that "I knew these writings were not inspired as Scripture is" (xii), she still desired "to share some of the messages I have received" (xiii). There is simply no way around it: Sarah Young is claiming to have received these messages directly from God. Whether or not you formally place those messages in the same category of Scripture, she is claiming to be a modern prophetess, receiving the Lord's word and transmitting it to others.

Friends, this is dangerous. We cannot say "thus saith the Lord" without considering the incredible weight of that responsibility, the closed canon of Scripture, and the fearful judgment promised to those who falsely claim to speak for God and/or add to His Word." – Rick Thomas' Review of

Jesus Calling (https://rickthomas.net/jesus-calling/)

You can't say it is wrong. Her intentions were good.

Some of the people I've discussed *Jesus Calling* with have responded, *"But her [Sarah Young] intentions are good."*

Jesus does not judge based on intentions. We can be Christians with good intentions and still be teaching falsehoods. In the Sermon on the Mount Jesus reveals that even believers can disobey God, and teach others to do the same.

> *Whoever then annuls one of the least of these commandments, and teaches others to do the same, shall be called least in the kingdom of heaven; -* Matthew 5:19

Notice that the penalty the false teacher receives is to be *"called least in the kingdom of heaven."* That means Jesus is talking about someone who is saved. They are in the kingdom, so they are a believer. But, they are teaching people to violate God's commandments. They are probably very sincere about what they are teaching, but it is still false teaching.

So we see from scripture that even true believers can present false teaching... lies... and they can be very sincere in their teaching. Does that make the false teaching acceptable? No. The good intentions of the teacher make no difference. If what is written is false, the good intentions of an author make no difference. You can be very sincere, and be very wrong.

What is written in *Jesus Calling* are not the words of Jesus. This is God we are talking about! God does not lend His name to be used to make a book more interesting. Any book that puts words in the mouth of God (Jesus), other than the words of scripture, is giving those words authority they do not deserve. That is very dangerous, and it makes this a book a book Christians should not be reading.

This IS NOT Jesus speaking. It IS NOT Jesus calling.

CHAPTER 4
SARAH YOUNG'S
NEW YORK TIMES INTERVIEW

Leading Christians have spoken or written about the problem of putting words in the mouth of Jesus, as has been done in *Jesus Calling*.

Personally... I would abandon it immediately. If she claims to be speaking Jesus' words, I am no longer interested. - Tim Challies (http://tiny.cc/5tnw4x)

It's written in the first person for Jesus. "I, Jesus, will do these things. I am such-and-such, I know this." Writes in the first person for Jesus. When you read it, it's a very warm, fuzzy, emotional effeminate Jesus. Ladies are eaten up with this. There's a shocking lack of discernment in the church today, shocking lack of discernment." - Justin Peters (http://tiny.cc/v3tq4x)

I find Jesus Calling troublesome, and would not recommend it...I'm stuck on the fact that Young is selling these words as if they were God's words. And that (as R. C. Sproul often says) "is a serious theological no-no." - Cripplegate, August 22, 2012 (http://tiny.cc/msb34x)

Has Sarah Young attempted to answer the claim that it is wrong to put words in Jesus' mouth? I could only find one article that addresses this. It is an October 25, 2013 article in the NY Times, called *"A First-Person Defense of Writing in Jesus' Voice."* To get an answer, the NY Times writer interviewed both Sarah Young and her editor. (The article is available at: http://tiny.cc/p5tq4x).

The article quotes Sarah Young's editor at Thomas Nelson books, Kris Bearss, as stating that Ms. Young's critics just do not understand the nuances of her project. Quoting the NY Times article:

> *"It's one thing for a person to relay what they feel that they have learned or gained through reading Scripture and prayer, and through time with the Holy Spirit,"* Ms. Bearss said. *"It's another thing for people to turn that into her saying that she is writing a new version of Scripture or that she is speaking for the Lord. That's not the case."*

Okay, let's take this statement at face value: she says *Jesus Calling* is not scripture. Ms. Bearss also says that *Jesus Calling* is what Sarah Young feels she has *"learned or gained through reading Scripture and prayer, and through time with the Holy Spirt."* That's interesting. This is not how Sarah Young described her experiences in the original introduction to *Jesus Calling*. But, putting that contradiction aside, Ms. Bearrs is clearly stating that what is in *Jesus Calling* are not the words of the Jesus, and *Jesus Calling* is not scripture.

So, if it is not scripture, why is it written as though it is scripture? To have God speaking these devotions is to directly imply they are scripture. When Jesus speaks, 100% of what He says is scripture.

The article then quotes Sarah Young. (Note: Sarah Young is responding to a questions sent to her via email.)

> *"I agree that revelation has ceased in the sense that the Bible is complete,"* Ms. Young wrote. *"However, what I am doing is devotional writing, and I do so by asking Jesus to guide my mind as I spend time with Him—to help me think His thoughts."*

What Sarah Young seems to be saying is that God guides her thoughts so that she is thinking the thoughts God wants her to think. But, because she is writing a devotional, when she writes down those thoughts as coming from the lips of Jesus, they are not scripture.

Does that make sense? No.

To pray and ask God to guide our thoughts and actions is a good thing. I hope you pray this way. I ask God to guide me when I am working on each week's sermon. I'm asking God to guide me as I write this book. And at times good ideas and phrases pop into my head—they just seem to come out of nowhere. Sometimes a Biblical concept or teaching suddenly becomes clear. I don't know if these are from God, or are the result of my own studying and thoughts. I do know that God is answering my prayers. But, that does not give me the liberty to write my sermons, nor this book, as though God was speaking.

By the way, here is a thought that just popped into my mind. Who is the helper sent to teach us and help us understand scripture? Who's "job" is it to guide our thoughts, when God desires them to be guided? Is it Jesus? No, it is the Holy Spirit. One of the roles of the Holy Spirit is to be the helper who guides and teaches us:

I will ask the Father, and He will give you another Helper, that He may be with you forever. - John 14:16

But the Helper, the Holy Spirit, whom the Father will send in My name, He will teach you all things, and bring to your remembrance all that I said to you. - John 14:26

But I tell you the truth, it is to your advantage that I go away; for if I do not go away, the Helper will not come to you; but if I go, I will send Him to you. - John 16:7

Who is the helper sent to teach us and help us understand scripture?

Jesus or the Holy Spirit?

Since it is the Holy Spirit who guides us, teaches us, and helps us, would it not be better for *Jesus Calling* to be written such that it was the Holy Spirit speaking? That would still be blasphemy, but it would be closer to what the Bible teaches.

What does it mean to *think God's thoughts after Him*?

In the NY Times article Sarah Young states that she asks, *"Jesus to guide my mind as I spend time with Him— to help me think His thoughts."* What does scripture say about thinking the thoughts of God? We can never fully comprehend the thoughts of God:

> For My thoughts are not your thoughts, nor are your ways My ways,"
> declares the Lord. "For as the heavens are higher than the earth, so are My
> ways higher than your ways and My thoughts than your thoughts.
> - Isaiah 55:8-9

There is a familiar saying: "*thinking God's thoughts after Him.*" Is this what Sarah Young is talking about? Is this a Biblical; saying? No, it is not from the Bible. This is a quote from Johannes Kepler (1571-1630) in which he was describing science as "*thinking God's thoughts after Him.*" What this means is that as science reveals more about the physical world, we learn more about God. Our understanding of God grows as our knowledge of our world grows.

Does the Bible say anything about thinking God's thoughts?

No, not directly. However, there are passages that indicate we should be thinking God's thoughts. We are created in the image of God, so we should only be thinking thoughts that God would think. Our thoughts can never be as deep and comprehensive as God's thoughts (Isaiah 55:8-9), but our thoughts should be in complete alignment with God's character. This is what it means to think God's thoughts.

> And do not be conformed to this world, but be transformed by the renewing of
> your mind, so that you may prove what the will of God is, that which is good
> and acceptable and perfect. - Romans 12:2

1st Corinthians chapter 2 says we have the Holy Spirit to guide us, and He reveals the thoughts of God through scripture, what Paul refers to as the "things freely given by God."

> The thoughts of God no one knows except the Spirit of God. Now we have
> received, not the spirit of the world, but the Spirit who is from God, so that we
> may know the things freely given to us by God. – 1 Corinthians 2:11b-12

The Holy Spirit is God, and knows the depth of God and the thoughts of God. The Holy Spirit is also the author of scripture. John

MacArthur writes:

"The process of the Spirit's transmission of God's truth is called inspiration. His truth cannot be discovered by man; it can only be received. In order to be received, something must first be offered. God's truth can be received because it is freely given. The Spirit who is from God, not the spirit of the world (that is human wisdom) has brought God's Word—which comprises the things freely given us by God. The Bible is the Spirit's vehicle for bringing God's revelation." – John MacArthur, The MacArthur New Testament Commentary 1 Corinthians, 1984, pages 62 and 63.

How is this accomplished? What do we need to do?

A.W. Tozer writes: *"To think God's thoughts requires much prayer. If you do not pray much, you are not thinking God's thoughts. If you do not read your Bible much and often and reverently, you are not thinking God's thoughts. Those thoughts you are having—and your head buzzes with them all day long and into the night—are earthly thoughts—thoughts of a fallen race. They are the thoughts of a lost society. They should not be our thoughts."* - Tozer Devotional, Cultivating Spiritual Disciplines (http://tiny.cc/m1vq4x)

Tozer then goes on to urge his readers to be in scripture. To think the thoughts of God your mind must be saturated with scripture.

"We ought to learn to live in our Bible... Begin with the Gospel of John, then read the Psalms. Isaiah is another great book to help you and lift you. When you feel you want to do it, go on to Romans and Hebrews and some of the deeper theological books. But get into the Bible. Do not just read the little passages you like, but in the course of year or two see that you read it through." - Tozer Devotional, Cultivating Spiritual Disciplines (http://tiny.cc/m1vq4x)

There's the answer. To think God's thoughts, you need to live in your Bible... constantly be in the Word of God. Saturate yourself with God's Word.

Although Sarah Young may be doing this, she never mentions it. She does say that *"I knew God communicated to me through the Bible,"* but then she follows that with, *"but I yearned for more."* Implying that scripture was not sufficient. She needed more than what God provided in the Bible. Apparently, instead of going deeper into the Word as Tozer recommends, she preferred going directly to God to receive *"personal messages from God."* That's not what scripture tells us to do. (The above quotes, in italics, are from the Introduction to the 2004 edition of *Jesus Calling*, page xii)

Let the word of Christ [scripture] richly dwell within you,
- Colossians 3:16

All Scripture is inspired by God and profitable for teaching, for reproof, for correction, for training in righteousness; so that the man of God may be adequate, equipped for every good work. — 2 Timothy 3:16-17

What about the devotions she wrote? Do they recommend that you saturate yourself in the Word of God? Again the answer is no. If anything, I'd say that *Jesus Calling* pretty much ignores reading the word as a spiritual discipline. The result of not being saturated with God's Word will be that you'll move further away from thinking God's thoughts.

The *Jesus Calling* devotional is not truly Jesus calling. The true Jesus is calling you to be in the Word. To turn to scripture... read your Bible... dive deep into scripture... and as a result you'll be going deep into God's thoughts and will learn to "think God's thoughts."

To get a free copy of the Gospel of John, go to:
http://www.livingwater.org

CHAPTER 5
ISN'T SCRIPTURE SUFFICIENT?

"I knew God communicated with me through the Bible, **but I yearned for more.** *Increasingly, I wanted to hear what God had to say to me personally on a given day. I decided to listen to God with pen in hand, writing down whatever I believed He was saying."* - Jesus Calling Introduction, 2004, page XII (bold emphasis added)

Does anything about this statement bother you?

Sarah Young is saying the Bible is not sufficient... she yearned for more. Is there more? Are there things, not included in scripture, which we need God to reveal to us directly? If there is more, why didn't God tell us to listen for His voice to give us further instructions? Instead God tells us in scripture not to look for more... we are not to add to or take away from what God has given us in scripture (Deuteronomy 4:2, Proverbs 30:6, Revelation 22:19).

Sarah Young is saying the "more" she needed was given to her directly by God. In her words in the original introduction to *Jesus Calling*, she said listened to God and wrote down what she believed He was saying. And she has shared that "more" with you through the book *Jesus Calling*.

Later in the same introduction Sarah Young tells you that scripture may not sufficient for you. But, she says, with the help of the *Jesus Calling* book, you may also receive thoughts or impression. It is implied that these thoughts and impressions would be from God, in the same way Sarah Young received messages from God. Note, the following does not say "thoughts or impressions you have," it says "thoughts or impressions you **receive**." These are not coming from you, you are receiving them. Here is the final paragraph of the introduction in the 2004 edition says:

> *"These messages* [the Jesus Calling book] *are meant to be read slowly, preferably in a quiet place. I invite you to keep a journal to record any thoughts or impressions you receive as you wait in His Presence."* - Jesus Calling Introduction, 2004, page XIV

This is not what the Bible says. Scripture is sufficient.

2 Timothy says that scripture, meaning the Bible, is all we need. It provides everything needed for us to be equipped for every good work... meaning everything God wants us to do.

> *All Scripture is inspired by God and profitable for teaching, for reproof, for correction, for training in righteousness; so that the man of God may be adequate, equipped for every good work.* – 2 Timothy 3:16-17

Read the above carefully. Does it say we are equipped by scripture for some things? No. Nothing else is needed. We are equipped for EVERY good work. Proverbs 30:5 & 6 says:

> *Every word of God is pure; He is a shield to those who put their trust in Him. Do not add to His words, Lest He rebuke you, and you be found a liar.* (NKJV)

In the Introduction to the 2004 edition of *Jesus Calling* Sarah Young writes:

> *This practice of listening to God has increased my intimacy with Him more than any other spiritual discipline, so **I want to share some of the messages I have received**. In many parts of the world, Christians seem to be searching for a deeper experience of Jesus' Presence and Peace. **The messages** that follow address that felt need.* – Jesus Calling, 2004 edition, page XIII, the bold emphasis is mine.

She says she is sharing messages she has received from God. So she is saying that scripture alone is not sufficient. In order to have the complete story, we need to hear directly from God... and the *Jesus Calling* book is the "more" that God had to say. It is the additional information that God did not include in the scripture.

WARNING! WARNING! Any time someone tells you that additional revelation is needed, that is a sure sign you are moving into the realm of false teaching. For example, the Mormons and Jehovah's Witnesses, both needed additional revelation.

There is a question I think will help clarify this: Does God still speak to us today? If so, how does He do this? Is it by putting messages in your head, as described by Sarah Young? Or does God have other ways of communicating with us?

The answer is, yes, God speaks to us today. But, God is not speaking in the same way He spoke through the Old Testament prophets, nor in the same way He spoke through the New Testament Apostles.

I've had some people tell me, *"God can do anything. That means He could speak to me directly."*

That is almost a correct statement, but it leaves out something. God can do anything **that is not a violation of His character**. And that means God, if He chose to, can speak through prophets today and could even give messages directly to every individual on the planet. But, just because God can do something, that does not mean He is doing it.

Before the Bible was complete God spoke through prophets and apostles. But, you won't read in scripture about Him speaking to

Depend on His perfect, complete, and infallible word in the Bible...

NOT your own fallible thoughts and senses.

everyday, individual people. And with the Bible now complete, a statement such as that in 2 Timothy can be made: scripture provides all we need to be equipped for every good work. This statement is telling us there is nothing more we need. No additional scripture is needed. Now that we have the complete Bible, Prophets and apostles are no longer needed. And personal messages from God were never needed. The Bible gives us everything we need to be thoroughly equipped.

God wants us to depend on His perfect, complete, and infallible Word in the Bible. He does not want us to depend on our own fallible thoughts and senses. He most definitely does not want us depending on what **we think** He might be saying to us, as Sarah Young says she did.

Does scripture ever tell us to trust our thoughts or to trust our senses (such as hearing or seeing messages from God)? No, never! Scripture tells us our heart, meaning our inner self, including our mind and thoughts, is deceitful and cannot be trusted:

The heart is more deceitful than all else and is desperately sick;
- Jeremiah 17:9

How do we know truth about God? We have the Spirit to guide us and help us understand scripture. But, the Spirit works by giving us an understanding of scripture, not by giving us messages. And in many cases that understanding only comes after saturating ourselves with God's Word, combined with hard hours of studying commentaries and other resources.

What are we to trust?

We are to trust God and God's Word. For example, we are to trust the promises God has given us in scripture, such as this promise that His promises are sufficient for us to become partakers of His divine nature:

For by these He has granted to us His precious and magnificent promises, so that by them you may become partakers of the divine nature, having escaped the corruption that is in the world by lust. — 2 Peter 1:4

We are to trust God, to supply all our needs:

And my God will supply all your needs according to His riches in glory in Christ Jesus. — Philippians 4:19

Does this mean we sit around and wait for people to bring us free food? No! In most cases He provides by giving us the ability to do a job so we can earn money to buy the food we need. That's why Paul writes that, if we don't work, we don't eat (1 Thessalonians 3:10).

We are also to trust God for our salvation, as described in scripture:

> *But in all these things we overwhelmingly conquer through Him who loved us. For I am convinced that neither death, nor life, nor angels, nor principalities, nor things present, nor things to come, nor powers, nor height, nor depth, nor any other created thing, will be able to separate us from the love of God, which is in Christ Jesus our Lord.* - Romans 8:37-39

Jesus Calling asks you to trust the messages Sarah Young "believes" resulted from God guiding her thoughts. *Jesus Calling* asks you to believe scripture is not sufficient and that Jesus has additional things to teach you. Don't believe it! The truth is, you are to trust the perfect Word of God, which is complete and provides all you need.

> *The law of the LORD is perfect, restoring the soul;*
> *The testimony of the LORD is sure, making wise the simple.*
> *The precepts of the LORD are right, rejoicing the heart;*
> *The commandment of the LORD is pure, enlightening the eyes.*
> *The fear of the LORD is clean, enduring forever;*
> *The judgments of the LORD are true; they are righteous altogether.*
> *They are more desirable than gold, yes, than much fine gold;*
> *Sweeter also than honey and the drippings of the honeycomb.*
> *Moreover, by them Your servant is warned;*
> *In keeping them there is great reward.* – Psalm 19:7-11:

> *So we have the prophetic word made more sure, to which you do well to pay attention as to a lamp shining in a dark place, until the day dawns and the morning star arises in your hearts. But know this first of all, that no prophecy of Scripture is a matter of one's own interpretation, for no prophecy was ever made by an act of human will, but men moved by the Holy Spirit spoke from God.* – 2 Peter 1:19-21

The *Jesus Calling* devotional book IS NOT JESUS CALLING. Trust the Bible. Scripture is complete and is sufficient.

CHAPTER 6
WHAT IS SPIRITUAL LEADING?

Could *Jesus Calling* be the result of spiritual leading?

Sarah Young has Jesus speaking the words in *Jesus Calling*. But is that the role Jesus has in the Trinity? Is He the one who guides and teaches us? Not according to scripture. Jesus promised the Father would send the Holy Spirit, and promised that the Holy Spirit would guide us and teach us.

> *I will ask the Father, and He will give you another Helper, that He may be with you forever; that is the Spirit of truth, whom the world cannot receive, because it does not see Him or know Him, but you know Him because He abides with you and will be in you.* - John 14:16-17

We have the Holy Spirit to teach us, to help us, and to encourage us. The Holy Spirit helps us understand God's word, and He clears the way for our spiritual growth. And, this is important, everything the Holy Spirit does is centered on Christ. The main role of the Holy Spirit is to point us to and glorify Christ. The focus is always on Jesus Christ.

> *When the Helper comes, whom I will send to you from the Father, that is the Spirit of truth who proceeds from the Father, He will testify about Me.* – John 15:26

A term Christians use to describe the work of the Holy Spirit is

34

"spiritual leading." Might not Sarah Young have been experiencing a spiritual leading? Might not the Holy Spirit be guiding her to have certain thoughts, and then she put those thoughts into writing?

How does the Holy Spirit guide us?

Everything
the
Holy Spirit
does is
centered on
CHRIST

Guidance from the Holy Spirit comes in subtle ways. We are not puppets God controls, God desires for us to be who we are, while at the same time growing and learning to be like Jesus. That means the Holy Spirit teaches us, and He also allows us to make our own decisions and mistakes. We often learn more from our mistakes than we'd learn if everything went perfectly.

What are some of the ways the Holy Spirit guides and teaches us? One way is through our conscience.

I am telling the truth in Christ, I am not lying, my conscience testifies with me in the Holy Spirit, – Romans 9:1 – (NASB)

The Holy Spirit also helps us by interceding with God on our behalf:

In the same way the Spirit also helps our weakness; for we do not know how to pray as we should, but the Spirit Himself intercedes for us with groanings too deep for words; – Romans 8:26

When we are in a difficult situation because of Christ, the Holy Spirit will teach us what to say:

When they bring you before the synagogues and the rulers and the authorities, do not worry about how or what you are to speak in your defense, or what you are to say; for the Holy Spirit will teach you in that very hour what you ought to say. – Luke 12:11-12

How does the Holy Spirit do this? Is it through our finding a beautiful, quiet place, clearing our minds of troubling thoughts, and focusing our thoughts on God, as described in *Jesus Calling*? Does God then guide our thoughts so that we receive and understand messages from Him? No, that's not how the Spirit works. There are exactly zero examples of ordinary individuals in scripture receiving direct revelation.

Not only is this not how the Holy Spirit works, scripture warns us against this! While going to a quiet place to pray can be good, clearing our minds and waiting for God to fill them with His thoughts is not Biblical. We are to fill our minds with scripture, not empty them.

And, should we receive a spiritual leading, it does not result in a series of messages such as those in *Jesus Calling*. A spiritual leading is most often experienced as an urging, an overwhelming desire, a feeling of peace, or a strong conviction that some sort of action is required or not required.

In addition, we have options: we can ignore a spiritual leading or act on it (1 Thessalonians 5:19). It is our choice, and it is one of the ways the Holy Spirit uses to teach us to make the right choices.

How can you tell the difference between a true spiritual leading, and personal intuition or desire?

It is very difficult to discern a spiritual leading from our own thoughts and desires. The only way it might be possible to do this is to be in the Word of God and thoroughly know the Word of God. If the "spiritual leading" is 100% in agreement with scripture, then it may be a true spiritual leading. If there is any doubt, if there is only 99% agreement with scripture, then it is probably your flesh speaking, not a spiritual leading.

By the way, if what you are experiencing are your own thoughts the same test applies. If they are 100% in agreement with scripture, then they are okay. It does not mean you are experiencing a spiritual leading, but it does mean that thought or idea is in accordance with the character of God. Always do as the Bereans did, test yourself, and if there is any doubt, assume the thought is not Biblical.

Now these were more noble-minded than those in Thessalonica, for they received the word with great eagerness, examining the Scriptures daily to see whether these things were so. - Acts 17:11

As you can see in the following two diagrams, determining whether a "spiritual leading" comes from the Holy Spirit or from ourselves is actually of no importance. We should not be focusing on trying to determine if a "leading" is from the Spirit. Our focus should be on the Word. We should determine whether "the leading" is in accordance with scripture.

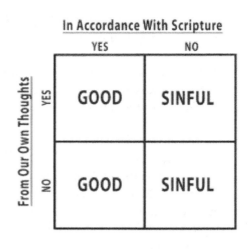

Are the devotions in *Jesus Calling* in agreement with scripture?

The claim is that these devotions are based on messages received from God, as God guided Sarah Young's thoughts. To claim that level of authority means the *Jesus Calling* devotions must be 100% in agreement with scripture.

Anything less than 100% agreement with scripture means *Jesus Calling* is not from God.

Scripture repeatedly warns us that a small sin, a little lie, poisons the whole batch... or in this case the whole book. Satan loves to lead us astray with small lies planted among truth. Scripture often uses the example of a small amount of yeast (leaven) spreading through all the dough:

> *Your boasting is not good. Don't you know that a little yeast leavens the whole batch of dough?* - 1 Corinthians 5:6

As we'll see in later chapters *Jesus Calling* has more than a small amount of "yeast." It includes a lot of false teaching.

> *You were running a good race. Who cut in on you to keep you from obeying the truth? That kind of persuasion does not come from the one who calls you. "A little yeast works through the whole batch of dough."*
> – Galatians 5:7-9

Earlier I said that, although the Spirit may be leading us, we can choose to ignore the Spirit and go our own way. That is true… God lets us make mistakes. When we ignore the Spirit, our flesh will lead us away from God. What does that mean? Even if *Jesus Calling* was the result of a Spiritual leading, that Spiritual leading was ignored. There is too much in *Jesus Calling* that is a violation of scripture.

Always remember to ask: does it agree with or conflict with scripture? If it conflicts with scripture, it is false teaching. If it presents a false Jesus or a false gospel, it is a false teaching. If it says something more than scripture is needed, it is false teaching.

> *Who is the liar but the one who denies that Jesus is the Christ?*
> – 1 John 2:22

> *Anyone who goes too far and does not abide in the teaching of Christ, does not have God;* - 2 John 9

In this chapter I tried to provide a beginner's level understanding of the role of the Holy Spirit. My point has been that, it doesn't matter whether you've had a Spiritual leading or your own thoughts are guiding you. What matters is whether or not it is 100% in agreement with scripture. So let's stop searching for Spiritual leadings, and start searching and diving deep into scripture.

As we'll see in Part II of this book, *Jesus Calling* is far from being fully in accordance with scripture. Even the scripture included with each devotion typically is used in a way that misleads the reader. *Jesus Calling* does not have the characteristics of a spiritual leading, nor does it have the scriptural soundness that is a part of anything that comes from God.

The *Jesus Calling* devotional book is not truly Jesus calling.

CHAPTER 7
GOD'S WORD DOES NOT CHANGE

Heaven and earth will pass away, but My words will not pass away. - Matthew 24:35

Understanding who God is immediately reveals problems with *Jesus Calling*. God is omniscient. He knows everything. God is perfect. He never makes a mistake. That means we can trust God. God has given us a number of promises, and we know we can depend on those promises because we know the character of God.

This also means that if God is communicating messages to someone, as claimed by Sarah Young, He will know a book will be published based on those messages (He is omniscient), and He will ensure that the messages are communicated clearly, correctly and completely, and that the resulting book is also correct.

He is God. He does not play guessing games with us. If He wishes to communicate messages that provide someone with "more" than what the Bible provides, then they will be communicated... completely, accurately, and clearly.

For God is not a God of confusion – 1 Corinthians 14:33

On the other hand, *Jesus Calling* has needed to be corrected, and the reason was that Sarah Young had Jesus saying things that contradicted scripture. Changes were made in the 10th Anniversary Edition, released in 2014, to correct conflicts with scripture and remove some of the more obvious New Age teaching. Here are some examples:

In the original 2004 edition, in two separate devotions, Jesus says that his last words before ascending into heaven were *"I am with you always."* However, His actual last words can be found in Acts 1:7 & 8:

> *"It is not for you to know times or epochs which the Father has fixed by His own authority; but you will receive power when the Holy Spirit has come upon you; and you shall be My witnesses both in Jerusalem, and in all Judea and Samaria, and even to the remotest part of the earth."* – Acts 1:7-8

For ten years what was published in *Jesus Calling,* as the last words spoken by Jesus, disagreed with what scripture said about Jesus' last words. The wording in the two original devotionals were:

January 28th (original 2004 edition): *I AM WITH YOU ALWAYS. These were the last words I spoke before ascending into heaven.*

October 15th (original 2004 edition): *TRY TO STAY CONSCIOUS OF ME as you go step by step through this day. My Presence with you is both a promise and a protection. My final statement just before I went to heaven was: Surely I am with you always.*

Millions of people have copies of *Jesus Calling* in which "Jesus" makes this incorrect statement about what He said in scripture. Jesus is God. Jesus does not make mistakes. This is not Jesus calling... a Jesus who needed to be corrected by changing *Jesus Calling* to the following:

January 28th (updated in 2014): *I AM WITH YOU ALWAYS. I spoke these words to My disciples after My resurrection.*

October 15th (updated in 2014): *TRY TO STAY CONSCIOUS OF ME as you go step by step through this day. My Presence with you is both a promise and a protection. After My resurrection, I assured My followers: Surely I am with you always.*

As mentioned in chapter one, Sarah Young claims she wrote what she believed Jesus was saying. So apparently what she believed she heard was wrong—in fact she got it wrong twice. Might she not have heard other things wrong? Might she have made other mistakes?

And incredibly, she incorrectly was guided by Jesus to think the wrong thoughts on two separate occasions! Or maybe the fault is hers, she incorrectly understood how Jesus was guiding her thoughts... and she incorrectly understood God's guidance in the same wrong way, on the same subject, on two separate occasions.

What a weak god Sarah Young has. A god who cannot ensure his message is communicated correctly.

By the way, if she had written this book differently, this would not be an issue. If she had said she was writing her thoughts, as other devotional writers do, then the need for corrections would be reasonable. But, that's not the claim made for *Jesus Calling*. These devotions are based on messages received from God as God guided the thoughts of Sarah Young. And they are written as though coming from the lips of Jesus.

"I decided to 'listen' with pen in hand, writing down whatever I 'heard' in my mind... This is how I was listening to Him—by focusing on Jesus and His word, while asking Him to guide my thoughts." - Jesus Calling, Introduction to the 2014 Anniversary Edition, page XII

"I decided to listen to God with pen in hand, writing whatever I believed He was saying. I felt awkward the first time I tried this, but I received a message." - Jesus Calling, 2004 edition, page XII

Let's look at just one more. How does scripture say we, as Christians, should feel about the physical circumstances in which we find ourselves? We should be content with whatever our circumstances are. You are to be content with whatever you have.

For I have learned to be content in whatever circumstances I am.
- Philippians 4:11

Make sure that your character is free from the love of money, being content with what you have; - Hebrews 13:5

Yet, in *Jesus Calling*, Jesus was not content with His birthplace. The original 2004 version, which was sold to millions of readers over a period of ten years, states:

Jesus speaking – December 25 (Original 2004 version): *"I accepted the limitations of infancy under the most appalling conditions—a filthy stable. That was a dark night for me..."*

Does this sound like Jesus speaking? Is our humble and loving God more concerned with earthly dirt than the sinful condition of humanity? The filth of sin is much worse than earthly dirt, and Jesus came to clean away the filth of sin.

On the other hand do the words in *Jesus Calling* sound more like something Satan might say? For whom was the night of Jesus' birth a "dark night?" Satan, of course. That night, the night the light of the world came into the world, was a very dark night indeed for Satan.

This sentence was changed in the 10th Anniversary edition to:

Jesus Speaking - December 25 (updated in 2014): *I accepted the limitations of infancy under the most appalling conditions—a filthy stable. There was nothing glorious about that setting.*

But, this still does not sound like the Jesus I know from scripture.

Of course, this can all be excused by saying, as Sarah Young has said, *Jesus Calling* is not scripture. So we should not expect it to perfect and it may need correcting. In that case, DON'T PUT WORDS IN JESUS' MOUTH THAT HE NEVER SAID! *Jesus Calling* has God saying things that are not true (based on scripture.) That is representing God as a liar. That is defaming the character of God! Don't do it!

I've shown two ways in which *Jesus* Calling needed to be corrected. There have been other corrections. The need for multiple corrections, to a book recording thoughts either received from, or guided by God, does not give me much confidence in what Sarah Young wrote. And even after the corrections, this book still does not sound like the real Jesus of the Bible.

This definitely is not the real Jesus calling. Jesus' words never need correcting.

CHAPTER 8
BUT, *JESUS CALLING* REALLY HELPED ME

For false Christs and false prophets will arise and will show great signs and wonders, so as to mislead, if possible, even the elect. – Matthew 24:24

Earlier this year I was talking about *Jesus Calling* with a woman named Beth. We talked about the many problems with *Jesus Calling*, and then she said, *"But, Jesus Calling has been so helpful to me. It helped me get through a very difficult time in my life."* No matter what I said, she was not going to give up reading *Jesus Calling*.

There is nothing wrong with something that helps you to feel good. God has given us feelings, and there is a purpose for our feelings. But, was it Jesus' purpose to come to earth to make us feel good? If so, shouldn't the words of Jesus in the Bible do the same things for us that *Jesus Calling* does? Shouldn't scripture give us the same type of fuzzy-warm, good feelings as *Jesus Calling* does? What's that, you say? Scripture doesn't make you feel like *Jesus Calling* makes you feel? There must be something wrong with scripture!

When talking about how they impact us, the difference between the Bible and *Jesus Calling* is that scripture deals with knowledge, understanding, and the promises of God. *Jesus Calling* deals with feelings and emotions.

Jesus Calling speaks to your emotions. It makes you feel good because it places you and your feelings at the center. The goal seems to be for you to stop worrying about your troubles, and have peaceful, comfortable, safe feelings because you are in the presence

43

of Jesus. That's a huge simplification, but that's what *Jesus* Calling is about… feelings and manipulating your emotions.

Is there anything wrong with feeling good? No, unless it leads you away from Jesus. And that's what *Jesus Calling* does. It places the focus on YOUR feelings. It is actually a book about you, not Jesus.

Here is the key question: Why are you reading *Jesus Calling?* Is it because you feel good when you read it? Or because it gives you a growing knowledge of God and His will? In his prayer for the Colossian church Paul shows us what the answer should be:

> *We have not ceased to pray for you and to ask that you may be filled with the knowledge of His will in all spiritual wisdom and understanding.* – Colossians 1:9

If your answer was that you read *Jesus Calling* because it makes you feel good, your focus is in the wrong place. It is on YOU, instead of

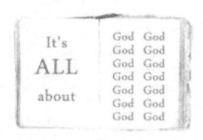

on GOD. It's a focus on making YOU feel good, not on growing closer to God through knowing Him better. Paul's prayer was for growing knowledge, not for the Colossians to have fuzzy-warm, comfortable feelings.

What is scripture about? God. Scripture focuses on God. It focuses on giving you knowledge about God… on what He has done, and on His plan for restoration and redemption. Does reading scripture result in feeling good? It should. But, that's not the purpose of scripture. It's the result of reading scripture… the result of learning about God, what He has done, and His promises.

> *Therefore we do not lose heart, but though our outer man is decaying, yet our inner man is being renewed day by day. For momentary, light affliction is producing for us an eternal weight of glory far beyond all comparison, while we look not at the things which are seen, but at the things which are not seen; for the things which are seen are temporal, but the things which are not seen are eternal.* - 2 Corinthians 4:16-18

Here is the key question for you to answer again: Why do you read your Bible? Is it because you feel good when you read it? Or because it gives you a growing knowledge of God and His will?

I hope you said you read the Bible to learn about God. Then your focus is on God, not yourself. Yes, scripture describes what God has done for us. We are filled with joy because of what He has done and what He has promised. Our hope is in His promises. But, the focus is always on God and what He has done, and not on you and making you feel good.

True teaching focuses on knowing God. False teaching focuses on the results of knowing God.

Yes, knowing God fills us with joy! Why are we filled with joy? One reason because, when we are saved, we become children of God and joint heirs with Christ, as Paul describes in Romans:

For as many as are led by the Spirit of God, these are sons of God. For you did not receive the spirit of bondage again to fear, but you received the Spirit of adoption by whom we cry out, "Abba, Father." The Spirit Himself bears witness with our spirit that we are children of God, and if children, then heirs; heirs of God and joint heirs with Christ, if indeed we suffer with Him, that we may also be glorified together. For I consider that the sufferings of this present time are not worthy to be compared with the glory which shall be revealed in us. For the earnest expectation of the creation eagerly waits for the revealing of the sons of God. - Romans 8:14-19

Where is Paul's focus? On God. As you read the above, what is it that we have done? Nothing. Why should we have joy when we are suffering? Because of God and His promise of eternal life. Because any suffering we experience now is nothing compared with partaking of the glory of God as an adopted child of God.

"A final truth about adoption is that it involves an inheritance....How unexpected and how breathtaking is the gracious provision of God! The marvel increases with the news that we are co-heirs with Christ. Sharing His sufferings may be looked at as simply the cost of discipleship. Yet it has a brighter aspect, because it is the prelude to partaking with Him of the coming glory." – Everett F. Harrison, Expositors Bible Commentary, 1986, Romans, page 93.

Does this focus on knowledge make the Bible seem rather dry and impersonal? Isn't God about relationships? Yes, He is. Have you noticed that in the Bible knowledge implies a relationship?

> *For the Christian, knowledge implies a relationship. For example, when the Bible says that "Adam knew Eve his wife" (Genesis 4:1, NKJV), it means he had a physical union with her. Spiritual relationships are also described this way. Jesus used the word know to refer to His saving relationship with those who follow Him: "I am the good shepherd; I know my sheep and my sheep know me" (John 10:14). He also told His disciples, "You will know the truth, and the truth will set you free" (John 8:32). By contrast, Jesus said to the unbelieving Jews, "You do not know [my Father]" (verse 55). Therefore, to know Christ is to have faith in Him, to follow Him, to have a relationship with Him, to love and be loved by Him. (See also John 14:7; 1 Corinthians 8:3; Galatians 4:9; and 2 Timothy 2:19.) Increasing in the knowledge of God is part of Christian maturity and is something all Christians are to experience as we "grow in the grace and knowledge of our Lord and Savior Jesus Christ" (2 Peter 3:18).* – Got Questions Ministry, http://tiny.cc/7uhb5x

If a book "helps" you, does that make it a good Christian book?

Reading a novel such as *A Tale of Two Cities* has helped some people get through a tough time. However, whether or not a book has "helped" you is not the criteria you should use to judge that book. There are web sites that recommend reading the Satanic Bible because some people feel it has helped them. Does that mean the Satanic Bible is a good book?

No!

The criteria we need to apply is: does it conform to scripture? Is it fully in agreement with scripture? It is in scripture that you'll find the answers that truly help you. It's amazing, scripture really does have the answers to all of our problems and troubles.

> *What then shall we say to these things? If God is for us, who is against us? He who did not spare His own Son, but delivered Him over for us all, how*

will He not also with Him freely give us all things? – Romans 8:31-32

What about emotional healing? Does the Bible have any answers? What does scripture say about healing when you are experiencing fear, anxiety, and depression? How can you overcome addictions?

The Bible has specific healing instructions for each of these, as well as every other emotional problem you could have. Yes, some problems are physical. If you are anxious and can't sleep, it may be because you've had 20 cups of coffee today. But, scripture does have the answers for all of your emotional problems. You will find the general principle in Ephesians chapter four:

So this I say, and affirm together with the Lord, that you walk no longer just as the Gentiles also walk, in the futility of their mind, being darkened in their understanding, excluded from the life of God because of the ignorance that is in them, because of the hardness of their heart; and they, having become callous, have given themselves over to sensuality or the practice of every kind of impurity with greediness.

But you did not learn Christ in this way, if indeed you have heard Him and have been taught in Him, just as truth is in Jesus, that, in reference to your former manner of life, you lay aside the old self, which is being corrupted in accordance with the lusts of deceit, and that you be renewed in the spirit of your mind, and put on the new self, which in the likeness of God has been created in righteousness and holiness of the truth. - Ephesians 4:17-24

Does this sound anything at all like *Jesus Calling?* No!! That's because this is the real deal... the real comfort... the real healing. This is God's word... the true Jesus calling!

Do you need to find a good Biblical counselor? Many counselors say they are "Biblical," but that does not mean they base their counseling on scripture. Look for a counselor who is certified by the Association of Certified Biblical Counselors (ACBC). More information is available on their web site:
www.biblicalcounseling.com

PART II – THE TRUTH
JESUS CALLING VS. SCRIPTURE

CHAPTER 9
DID I HEAR THAT RIGHT?

"I knew God communicated with me through the Bible, but I yearned for more. Increasingly, I wanted to hear what God had to say to me personally on a given day. I decided to listen to God with pen in hand, writing down whatever I believed He was saying." - Jesus Calling 2004, XII

I hope the word "believes" caught your attention. Sarah Young said that she wrote down *"whatever I believed He was saying."*

Does that mean there was some doubt? Was she not certain about how God was guiding her thoughts? Possibly God was trying to communicate something, and she was not hearing it correctly.

Is that possible? Who are we talking about here? God.

Does God play guessing games with us? No. Never.

The devotions in *Jesus Calling* are presented as authoritative, meaning we are to believe and do what they tell us to believe and do. These devotions are presented as something we should trust and act on. So, shouldn't we be concerned that, if Sarah Young was being guided by God and supposedly writing what He was saying, that she was correctly hearing God and correctly writing what He was saying?

But she writes that she "believed" she was writing down what God was saying.

If God wishes to communicate with us, can He make sure we clearly understand His message? Of course!

If God is giving us messages, as described in the introduction to *Jesus Calling*, would He not be sure we clearly understood those messages? Of course He would. It makes no sense for God to give a message, but not let us hear the message clearly and correctly. We can choose to ignore God, but He would at least communicate His message clearly.

And consider this... since Jesus knows that Sarah Young would write down His messages, and put them in a book over 15 million people would read, wouldn't He make sure His messages were clearly understood by her? You bet He would.

The God of the Bible is not weak and unable to communicate both perfectly and clearly. The God of the Bible is not a God of confusion (1 Corinthians 14:33), If He is communicating with someone, it will be perfectly communicated and be exactly the message God wants that person to hear. No mistakes. No questions about what they heard.

That's why God gives this test to determine if someone is really passing on messages that came from God.

> *When a prophet speaks in the name of the Lord, if the thing does not come about or come true, that is the thing which the Lord has not spoken.* - Deuteronomy 18:22.

Sarah Young does not claim to be a prophetess, and she specifically denies she is writing scripture. Yet, she claims to have written a devotional book based on messages from God... putting the words she wrote into the mouth of Jesus. You cannot claim that God would not know all of this in advance. And with God knowing this, certainly He would not allow any uncertainty or confusion about what He was communicating... if this was really from God.

If *Jesus Calling* was of God, something that God either said or guided Sarah Young to write (as claimed in a later edition), then He surely would have guided her to get it right. How could Jesus, if it was truly Jesus speaking, allow a book with errors (see chapters 9 through 15), and for which God's chosen author wasn't sure she was hearing Him correctly, to be written and published?

Sarah Young states that she wrote what she *BELIEVED* Jesus was saying. That's not a good sign. This can only happen if *Jesus Calling* was not from God... but no way could this happen if it was truly God guiding Sarah Young's thoughts. It never happens in scripture. Every one of the 40 people, who were involved in writing scripture, clearly understood what they were to write. God communicated clearly, the writers knew God was communicating clearly, and there were no misunderstandings or doubts. That's the way the real God... the real Jesus works.

Some of you may be thinking: *"This isn't fair. You are applying the standards for a prophet. Sarah Young does not claim to be a prophet."*

A prophet, or prophetess, is someone whom God has chosen as His messenger. Sarah Young said she was receiving messengers from God, and that God guided her thoughts, and that she passed those thoughts on to us through *Jesus Calling*, and various other books. She is certainly acting like a prophetess.

But, she doesn't need to call herself a prophetess. The label we apply to someone isn't important. We can tell who and what they are from their words and actions. So, without regard to what she calls herself, if God is going to give teaching through her—as is done in *Jesus Calling*—then God would communicate with her in such a way that His messages are communicated perfectly, remembered perfectly, and written down by her perfectly. That's what God does.

If God can put words in the mouth of a donkey (Numbers 22:28), and that donkey clearly and correctly delivers the message. Surely that same God can clearly and accurately put the words He desires into Sarah Young's thoughts and her book.

But the prophet who speaks a word presumptuously in My name which I have not commanded him to speak, or which he speaks in the name of other gods, that prophet shall die. – Deuteronomy 18:20

Sarah Young states that she wrote *"down whatever I believed He was saying."* She's not sure what she heard, yet she puts those words into the mouth of Jesus. That's not the way the God of the Bible works. Are you willing to trust in the Jesus of *Jesus* Calling, or do you trust the true Jesus of scripture?

By the way, which book are you spending more time in? *Jesus Calling* or the Bible? Many of the people I talk with say they are reading *Jesus Calling,* but not the Bible. They are choosing to spend their time with a false Jesus instead of the real Jesus. That's sad as well as disturbing. Those people are loving themselves and turning their backs on God. I beg you, be in God's word… His true word in the Bible.

The messages in *Jesus Calling* are not messages from God—these messages are not Jesus calling.

Next, let's begin taking a look at one of the *Jesus Calling* devotions and find out whether or not what "Jesus" is saying is Biblical.

> Do not say of any error, "It is a mere matter of opinion." No man indulges an error of judgment, without sooner or later tolerating an error in practise.
>
> -- Charles Spurgeon, Devotional Classics of C. H. Spurgeon, July 4th

CHAPTER 10
EXAMINING A *JESUS CALLING* DEVOTIONAL
PART A

Now these were more noble-minded than those in Thessalonica, for they received the word with great eagerness, examining the Scriptures daily to see whether these things were so. - Acts 17:11

Anytime someone has questioned me about *Jesus Calling*, I'd ask then to pick a day... any day. We'd then turn to the devotion for that day, and read it and the scripture references. Then we'd talk about what we read... not about the feelings it created, but what the devotion for that day actually said. In every case, no matter what day was randomly selected, the message was not a Biblical message. We'll do that beginning in the next chapter. But, before we look at a specific *Jesus Calling* devotion, we need to recognize an important characteristic of *Jesus Calling*:

Jesus Calling devotions typically have few specifics.

Let's play a game. For ten points can you identify which day in *Jesus Calling* this quote is from?

"There is only so much you can accomplish in a day. Set your priorities and work methodically to finish what you start. Doing too much for too many will lead to disappointment."

If you've read any of the *Jesus Calling* devotions this quote will sound familiar. But you may be having trouble recalling the specific date. Don't bother looking. The correct date is September 3, 2015... and it's from the astrology section of the daily newspaper (The Republican, Springfield, MA, September 3, 2015).

The *Jesus Calling* devotions are similar in many respects to horoscopes. Or, as my friend Wendi said, *"They are like fortune cookies."* They are worded in a way that is open to multiple interpretations. For example:

- If you are a conservative Christian, when you read *Jesus Calling* you will find that it is teaching conservative Christian principles. You will be reading into the devotion your understanding of scripture.

- If you are a liberal Christian, when you read *Jesus Calling* you will find that it is teaching progressive Christian principles. You will be reading into the devotion your understanding of scripture.

- The same thing applies to people who think they are Christian, but actually they are not. They will see their humanistic beliefs reflected in *Jesus Calling*.

That's what makes *Jesus Calling* so popular. Whatever you believe, you'll think that *Jesus Calling* is perfect. No matter what type of "Christian" belief you have, it will appear *Jesus Calling* supports your beliefs.

Whatever you believe, you'll think that Jesus Calling is perfect.

But, if you stop and think about what you are reading, taking it as literally as you do when reading a newspaper, what you'll typically get is a very different message than what you originally thought.

Here's what's going on: The *Jesus Calling* devotions are written as though they are speaking to your intellect... they seem to be providing practical advice from Jesus. But, that is deceptive.

There's the ol' switcheroo going on here. You think you are getting knowledge, but what you are actually getting is a boost to your self-esteem and a lot of good feelings. That's the deception. These devotions seem like they are speaking to your intellect, but they are actually speaking to your emotions.

That's why *Jesus Calling* is wildly popular with women, but men show limited interest. Women love *Jesus Calling*, and are loath to give it up because it speaks to their emotions in a way that makes them feel good.

BUT... is this why Jesus came? To make us feel good? Is this the message Jesus brings in scripture, one that makes us feel good about ourselves? No, that is not the purpose of God's word. Jesus brings truth... the truth Jesus brings is the gospel of salvation. For those who believe Jesus, the gospel brings great joy. A joy that can never be taken away by your circumstances. Joy that never ends.

For non-believers the truth Jesus brings sometimes results in anger and hatred. We saw this during Jesus' day. He was hated and despised by those who rejected Him, to the point that they crucified Him even though he was innocent. In His entire life He had never done anything wrong, yet He was crucified. His enemies thought crucifixion was the end... they had done away with this disturbing rabbi. But the cross was not the end, it was the beginning.

What was Jesus' message? What is the truth we all need to know? We've broken God's laws. Our conscience tells us this is true.

For all have sinned and fall short of the glory of God, - Romans 3:23

If we say that we have not sinned, we make Him a liar and His word is not in us. - 1 John 1:10

That means we have earned the penalty all law-breakers earn... eternity in the lake of fire (Revelation 21:8). But, 2000 years ago on the cross Jesus (God) paid the penalty we've earned in full. He died so that you can live. If you repent (turn away from law-breaking and turn toward obeying God), and trust that Jesus really did fully pay your penalty for sin... you are saved. You are saved from the wrath of God and you now have eternal life.

This is the truth Jesus preached. It is not an appeal to our emotions. It is not told just to make us feel good about ourselves. It is a factual statement giving us knowledge about the problem we all have (sin), and what God has done to save us from the consequences of sin.

This IS the reason God came to earth 2000 years ago.

But, God does not force you to do something you don't want to do. You can either believe it and be saved, or reject it and pay the penalty you've earned for sin.

For the Son of Man has come to seek and to save that which was lost. - Luke 19:10

The Son of Man did not come to be served, but to serve, and to give His life a ransom for many. - Matthew 20:28

For those who turn away from Jesus this is dreadfully bad news that brings no joy. For those who are trusting in Jesus Christ, this is the best news possible, and they are filled with joy.

But the fruit of the Spirit is love, joy, peace, patience, kindness, goodness, faithfulness, gentleness, self-control; against such things there is no law. - Galatians 5:22-23

Yes, there is great peace and joy in the gospel. But, Jesus' message is not about the joy it brings, it is not about emotion. It is ALL about solving the problem of sin. God's perfect creation was marred by sin (Genesis 3). The Bible is about God's restoration of His creation to perfection. Everything God has told us in scripture has been about sin and what God has done about it—praise and all glory be to God!

So that the proof of your faith, being more precious than gold which is perishable, even though tested by fire, may be found to result in praise and glory and honor at the revelation of Jesus Christ; and though you have not seen Him, you love Him, and though you do not see Him now, but believe in Him, **you greatly rejoice with joy inexpressible** *and full of glory, obtaining as the outcome of your faith the salvation of your souls.* - 1 Peter 1:7-9

Jesus Calling never talks about the inexpressible joy we have as a result of trusting Jesus Christ as our savior. *Jesus Calling* never mentions the problem we ALL have: sin... and the result: eternal punishment in hell. *Jesus Calling* never mentions what we need to do to be saved from hell: trust that Jesus paid our penalty for breaking God's laws (sin).

On the other hand, the real Jesus talks about hell twice as much as He talks about heaven. He talks about our being broken (sin) and tells us that it is only through Him that we can have restoration... it is only Jesus who gives salvation from the wrath of God. That is the important message God wants to communicate to us... we are broken sinners in need of a Savior. That is NOT what *Jesus Calling* is about.

Jesus Calling presents a very different Jesus from the Jesus of the Bible. The message in *Jesus Calling* in not the message the true Jesus brings to us... it is a fuzzy, nebulous message that speaks to your emotions. The Jesus of *Jesus Calling* is a Jesus who doesn't truly care about you... He doesn't care about your salvation... He doesn't care that you won't be with Him for eternity. The Jesus of *Jesus Calling* just wants you to feel good as you head to eternity in hell under God's wrath.

THIS IS NOT THE TRUE JESUS!

CHAPTER 11
EXAMINING A *JESUS CALLING* DEVOTION
PART B

What Does *Jesus Calling* Actually Say?

Let's look at an example – *Jesus Calling*, May 16ᵗʰ

The following was randomly selected, by someone asking me about the *Jesus Calling* book. This is from the original 2004 edition of Jesus Calling.

> *I AM YOUR LORD! Seek me as Friend and Lover of your soul, but remember that I am also King of kings—sovereign over all. You can make some plans as you gaze into the day that stretches out before you. But you need to hold those plans tentatively, anticipating that I may have other ideas. The most important thing to determine is what to do right now. Instead of scanning the horizon of your life, looking for things that need to be done, concentrate on the task before you and the One who never leaves your side. Let everything else fade into the background. This will unclutter your mind, allowing Me to occupy more and more of your consciousness.*

> *Trust Me to show you what to do when you have finished what you are doing now. I will guide you step by step as you bend your will to mine. Thus you stay close to me on the path of Peace.*

The two scripture references are: Proverbs 19:21 and Luke 1:79.

It Seems To Make Sense – At First

I've found that as I read a *Jesus Calling* devotion it sounds Biblical and it seems to makes sense... until I stop to carefully think about what it actually says compared with what scripture says.

There is some truth in some of the *Jesus* Calling devotions. But, a devotion with some truth is still not trustworthy. Always keep in mind, to be discerning you need to be able to discern the true from the almost true. The false teaching that brings death is almost always surrounded by truth. However, and this is important, the Bible tells us that a little leaven (false teaching) spreads through the entire dough—meaning a small bit of wrong teaching ruins the entire book. And, *Jesus Calling* has more than a little bit of leaven.

Six Steps for evaluating a *Jesus Calling* devotion

Step 1: The first question to ask is: what are the main themes of this devotion? What are the messages the devotion communicates? I usually find two or three messages in each day's devotion. For this example we're not going to dig that deep. We'll look at just the one message that appears to be the most significant for the day we are looking at.

To find the main themes read through the devotion several times, one sentence at a time, picking out the key points being made. Look for words that tell you what to do or think. Then break down each key point into its component parts, paying attention to the meaning of each word.

In this devotion one of the key points is expressed in the final sentence of the first paragraph: *"This will unclutter your mind, allowing Me to occupy more and more of your consciousness."* That seems like a good thing... having Jesus occupy more and more of your consciousness. So let's analyze this what is actually being said here.

Step 2: Next ask questions that will help you understand exactly what you are being told. Look to carefully define every word and every idea in the selected sentence. For example: According to *Jesus Calling,* what does it mean to unclutter your mind? What does it mean to allow Jesus to occupy more of your consciousness?

Keep in mind that different people will give different answers to these questions. What is written in *Jesus Calling* will mean different things to different people. The best you and I can do is to write down the answers we come up with.

To help you do this, it can be helpful to paraphrase what you think the selected teaching is saying. Here is my paraphrase: First unclutter your mind... then allow Jesus to occupy more and more of your thoughts.

Step 3: Next take the first part of the paraphrase and determine what, specifically, you need to do in order to obey this command from Jesus. For me, the command appears to be to get rid of all your distracting thoughts, just empty out your mind... clean it out. So the question is, what do you need to do to unclutter your mind? In some cases the devotion will have some instructions that are helpful. So read through the devotion again looking specifically for ways to unclutter your mind. Here is what I found:

> *"Instead of scanning the horizon of your life, looking for things that need to be done, concentrate on the task before you and the One who never leaves your side. Let everything else fade into the background."*

To understand what is being said, let's break down this command, making a list of what it is telling you to do. Here's the list:

1. Don't think about what you need to do in the future.
2. Concentrate on what you are doing now.
3. Concentrate on the Jesus of *Jesus Calling*.
4. Let everything but the present moment fade away.

Step 4: Based on the above list, ask more questions? Stop and think. Do you understand everything on the list?

The first question that comes to my mind is, *"What's this about not thinking about the future? Shouldn't we do some sort of planning for tomorrow?"* That's a good question, and we'll talk about it in the next chapter. (The answer is "yes" we should plan for the future.)

Another question that comes to my mind is: *"What would I most likely be doing 'now' that I need to concentrate on?"* That's numbers two and four on the above list. I'm being told to focus on just what I am doing now. So, what am I doing now? I'd be focusing on doing what *Jesus Calling* has told me to do: get rid of all my other thoughts and concentrate just on the "Jesus" of *Jesus Calling*—number three on the list. This is a command to empty your mind of everything and fill it with the false Jesus of *Jesus Calling*. Unclutter your mind. Focus on getting rid of all those other thoughts... make room for "Jesus."

This all sounds good. Very relaxing. But, what *Jesus Calling* is commanding you to do is the opposite of what scripture tells you to do. Don't empty your mind. Fill your mind with scripture. Fill your mind with God's Word. Then, when you are stuffed with scripture, dwell on all that is of good repute and worthy of praise. (You cannot discern what is "good" and praiseworthy until you are thoroughly familiar with scripture.)

> *Finally, brethren, whatever is true, whatever is honorable, whatever is right, whatever is pure, whatever is lovely, whatever is of good repute, if there is any excellence and if anything worthy of praise, dwell on these things.* — Philippians 4:8

Step 5: Take everything you've learned and find out what scripture says about what you've uncovered. For example, what does scripture say happens when you empty your mind? You leave yourself open for evil to move in. In Matthew 12 Jesus tells the story about a man from whom all evil spirits are cleaned out. Then the demon that was cleaned out says:

> *"I will return to my house from which I came;" and when it comes, it finds it unoccupied, swept, and put in order. Then it goes and takes along with it seven other spirits more wicked than itself, and they go in and live there; and the last state of that man becomes worse than the first.*
> - Matthew 12:44-45

When you are cleaned out... when you empty your mind... something will fill it... and most likely that something will not be good. The Bible never tells you to do what *Jesus Calling* says to do. Scripture never tells you to clean out your mind, you are told to renew your mind and fill it with scripture and good things. As you fill it with Godly thoughts, everything that is bad will be pushed out.

> *Set your minds on things that are above, not on things that are on earth.*
> — Colossians 3:2

This book of the law [scripture] *shall not depart from your mouth, but you shall meditate on it day and night...* - Joshua 1:8

Until I come, devote yourselves to the public reading of Scripture, to exhortation, to teaching. — 1 Timothy 4:13

What are you to fill your mind with? #1 on the list is God's Word. The *Jesus Calling* devotions never encourages you to be filled with the Word of God. You are to clean yourself out and wait for Jesus to fill you with "His presence." That's dangerous!! NO! Keep your mind filled with scripture so there is no place for the natural man or Satan.

Step 6: Now let's look at the next part of the selected sentence and repeat the process. Remember, do your best to take just what the words say. Here is our paraphrase: *"allow Jesus to occupy more and more of your thoughts."*

When you "allow" something to happen, that means you do nothing on your own. You just wait, and allow outside forces to act. So this *Jesus Calling* devotion is saying that you are to empty your mind of everything, except the present, then wait for something to fill it. Yikes! Red warning lights should be flashing!!

Is this Biblical? Not at all! This not Christianity. This is a New Age mystical religious practice. Empty your mind and wait for something to fill it, and this helps you become one with God. NO!

What does the Bible say to do? To fill your mind with the things of God. Fill your mind with scripture. That is the true Jesus calling! Calling you to be in His word. Calling you to fill your mind with His word. Stuff it full! Live His word.

Fill your mind,
your heart,
your soul,
your life
with
SCRIPTURE

CHAPTER 12
EXAMINING A *JESUS CALLING* DEVOTION
PART C

What about the scripture references in *Jesus Calling*?

Each *Jesus Calling* devotion typically includes two or three scripture references. On the surface the *Jesus Calling* scripture references may seem to support what *Jesus Calling* is teaching. But, when properly understood in their context, they often are not even related to the teaching in the associated *Jesus Calling* devotion.

In the previous chapter we looked at content of the May 16th *Jesus Calling* devotion (2004 edition). The two scripture references for May 16th are: Proverbs 19:21 and Luke 1:79. Let's start with Proverbs 19:21...

> ***Many are the plans in a person's heart, but it is the LORD's purpose that prevails.*** - Proverbs 19:21 -

Jesus Calling never explains the connection between the referenced verses and the content of the devotion. So we'll need to make some assumptions. The devotion talks about letting go of the future and just focusing on what you are doing now. So I assume Proverbs 19:21 was referenced because it seems to say that we should not rely on our own plans for the future because God's plans will prevail

Here is what the May 16th *Jesus Calling* devotion says:

You can make some plans as you gaze into the day that stretches out before you. But you need to hold those plans tentatively, anticipating that I may have other ideas. The most important thing to determine is what to do right now. Instead of scanning the horizon of your life, looking for things that need to be done, concentrate on the task before you and the One who never leaves your side. - Jesus Calling, 2004 Edition, May 16, page 143

As with most *Jesus Calling* devotions, at a first reading it sounds very good. "Jesus" is telling you to only make tentative plans for the future. You are to focus on what you are doing right now and on Jesus.

That you are to let go of the future and live for the present is a reoccurring theme in *Jesus Calling*. But, is that what Proverbs 19:21 is saying? NO!

What does scripture say about planning for the future?

In general, scripture tells us that we should plan and prepare for the future. However, we should plan with Godly wisdom, which comes from being in God's word.

Where there is no guidance, a people falls, but in an abundance of counselors there is safety. - Proverbs 11:14 (ESV)

The above proverb, as well as other scripture, tells us to get guidance from other people... from good counselors. This, of course, is part of planning. If you are not thinking about the future, there is no reason to get counsel from others.

So whoever knows the right thing to do and fails to do it, for him it is sin. - James 4:17

How do we know the right thing to do? By looking toward the future, looking at the options we have, and then choosing to do the right thing. We can only do this if we are planning for the future.

The plans of the diligent lead surely to abundance, but everyone who is hasty comes only to poverty. – Proverbs 21:5

Proverbs 21:5 straight out tells us to properly plan for the future. If we wait until the last minute and make hasty decisions, the outcome will not be good.

> *For which of you, desiring to build a tower, does not first sit down and count the cost, whether he has enough to complete it? Otherwise, when he has laid a foundation and is not able to finish, all who see it begin to mock him, saying, 'This man began to build and was not able to finish.' Or what king, going out to encounter another king in war, will not sit down first and deliberate whether he is able with ten thousand to meet him who comes against him with twenty thousand? And if not, while the other is yet a great way off, he sends a delegation and asks for terms of peace.*
> - Luke 14:28-33

If Proverbs 19:21 is not about planning for the future being of no value, what is it actually saying? The message is: the plans we make are always subject to God's sovereignty. God is in control. When taken in the context of all of scripture, the Bible plainly says: we are to make plans for the future, but with wisdom and humility. Scripture teaches against the two extremes. Doing no planning, and making and totally trusting your own plans. We are to plan for the future using Godly wisdom. If you are in God's Word... if you know God's Word and have a scripture-based understanding of God's will, then your plans will be in God's will. *Jesus Calling* never mentions this.

So what we have is *Jesus Calling* missing the mark. The point of Proverbs 19:21 is that God is sovereign. Is that the message you get from this devotion? It doesn't seem so. Its focus is on you, not on God. Jesus Calling says:

> *"The most important thing to determine is what to do right now."*

While that's not bad advice, it's not what Proverbs 19:21 says. This proverb is saying that it is important to know God... it is important to know that He is sovereign. Proverbs 19:21 is not about focusing on today, it is about keeping our focus on God.

What about the New Testament scripture reference?

...to shine on those living in darkness and in the shadow of death, to guide our feet into the path of peace. - Luke 1:79

This verse seems to have been picked because it refers to the *"path of peace."* The connection to the devotion is probably the final paragraph of the May 16th devotion, which refers to the path of peace:

> *Trust Me to show you what to do when you have finished what you are doing now. I will guide you step by step as you bend your will to mine. Thus you stay close to me on the path of Peace.* – Jesus Calling, 2004 Edition, May 16, page 143

What *Jesus Calling* seems to be referring to is finishing what you have to do today, and then let Jesus guide you. If you trust Jesus to guide you, then you don't need to worry about tomorrow. Your mind will be at peace because you've put Jesus in control, and you are on the path to peace.

What is Luke 1:79 talking about? What is the true, scriptural path of peace?

The context of Luke 1:79 is that of the coming Messiah and salvation. It is a prophecy about Jesus saving us. So this verse is not for believers, it is a verse for non-believers. Believers do not need to be on the path to peace, because we already have peace. It is the non-believer who needs to be on the path to peace.

The "peace" of *Jesus Calling* appears to be a peace of "no troubles." In other words, if you have no troubles and no worries about the future, you'll have peace.

What is the path of peace referred to in Luke 1:79? It is the path to repentance and trusting Jesus for having paid the penalty you've earned as a result of breaking God's laws. The path to peace is the path to salvation. We can only have peace, when we are saved. And when we are saved we have peace.

That is nothing like what *Jesus Calling* is talking about. Luke is talking about God guiding non-believers into the path to salvation. There is no mention of sin (the darkness Luke mentions), nor the penalty for sin (the death Luke mentions).

Notice that in the quote from *Jesus Calling* Jesus will guide you in bending your will to Jesus' will. By doing this you will be able to stay close to Jesus on the path to peace of not worrying about the future.

The Bible never talks about non-believers slowly bending their will to Jesus. That's something they can't do. Unless someone is saved, they are totally outside the will of Jesus. The only option is to give up your pride—what scripture calls being poor in spirit—and trust Jesus.

However, let's assume the referenced verse may is not intended to be related to the topic of the devotion, and the devotion is actually about believers. Maybe the "Jesus" in *Jesus Calling* is talking about BELIEVERS bending their will to conform to His will. Then might this be talking about the process of sanctification… growing to be more like Jesus?

Is this how scripture describes conforming your mind to that of Jesus? No, not even close. Scripture tells us to put off the old man and put on the new. We are not to take the old, our worldly mind, and try to bend it to conform to God's requirements. We are to be transformed by putting on the new… we are given a new heart and new desires. We don't bend the old, we put on the new.

> *Therefore, God's chosen ones, holy and loved, put on heartfelt compassion, kindness, humility, gentleness, and patience, accepting one another and forgiving one another if anyone has a complaint against another. Just as the Lord has forgiven you, so you must also forgive. Above all, put on love—the perfect bond of unity. And let the peace of the Messiah, to which you were also called in one body, control your hearts.* – Colossians 3:12-15

Notice that Paul mentions *"let the peace of the Messiah….control your hearts."* This is a peace you already have. A peace that comes with salvation. Unlike what *Jesus Calling* says, as a believer you do not need to be on the path to peace, you already have the peace of Jesus.

> *And do not be conformed to this world, but be transformed by the renewing of your mind, so that you may prove what the will of God is, that which is good and acceptable and perfect.* – Romans 12:2

Jesus Calling and scripture are teaching different things. Keep in mind this was a randomly selected devotion. Similar non-Biblical teaching is found in most *Jesus Calling* devotions.

For those who want to go a little deeper, let's look at the details of Luke 1:79.

This verse is from Zachariah's Song of Salvation. It's about the three covenants, and in particular salvation through the New Covenant. It is about the Messiah who is to *"to shine on those living in darkness and in the shadow of death, to guide our feet into the path of peace."*

Luke 1:79 is talking about the Messiah and the light of salvation. This is not a verse that gives everyday guidance to believers as implied in *Jesus Calling*. It is about lost sinners stumbling around in darkness knowing nothing of true peace (Romans 3:17). Knowing nothing about the peace comes from a right relationship with God (John 14:27). Knowing nothing about the peace begins with salvation (Romans 5:1). Knowing nothing of the peace that is one of the fruits of the Spirit (Galatians 5:22).

The May 16th *Jesus Calling* devotion implies that as believers we can be on the path to peace, if we trust Jesus with all our cares and worries. The Biblical truth is that as believers we already have peace. We are not on the path to peace. We have arrived! What we need to do is use that peace to control any unrest that is in our hearts.

The moment when you are saved you are united with Christ and are at peace with God. It is finished.

Although *Jesus Calling* includes scripture, that scripture does not support the teaching of *Jesus Calling*. Just including scripture does not make a book Biblical. Satan used scripture when tempting Jesus... or I should say he did as *Jesus Calling* does... he misused scripture.

Jesus Calling is definitely NOT the real Jesus calling.

CHAPTER 13
HOW CAN I EXPERIENCE
THE PRESENCE OF JESUS?

"I first experienced the Presence of God in a setting of exquisite beauty. ... I went into a deeply wooded area, feeling vulnerable and awed by cold, moonlit beauty. The air was crisp and dry, piercing to inhale. Suddenly I felt as if a warm mist enveloped me. I became aware of a lovely Presence, and my involuntary response was to whisper, 'Sweet Jesus.'" - Jesus Calling introduction, pages VI & VII, 2004 unrevised edition.

"When I prayed for myself, I was suddenly enveloped in brilliant light and profound peace. I lost all sense of time as I experienced God's presence in this powerful way." - Jesus Calling introduction, pages X & XI, 2004 unrevised edition.

What is the overall theme of the *Jesus Calling* book? Its full title is, *"Jesus Calling, Enjoying Peace In His Presence."* Based on the title I assume there is a focus on experiencing the presence of Jesus (God). And that is what we see when we read this book. Just in the introduction *Jesus Calling* speaks about the presence of God 19 times.

When we read the *Jesus Calling* devotions we find the same focus on being in the presence of Jesus. I randomly picked a date, which turned out to be October 13th, and I counted the number of times being in the presence of Jesus is mentioned in the next ten devotions. It was 18 times. In addition, phrases that imply the presence of Jesus, such as *"aware of my companionship,"* are commonly used.

Experiencing the presence of Jesus is a huge part of this book. So let's find out what *Jesus Calling* means when it talks about being in the presence of Jesus. We'll also look at the true Biblical meaning of being in the presence of Jesus.

According to *Jesus Calling*, what does it mean to be in the presence of Jesus?

In *Jesus Calling* the presence of Jesus seems to be a feeling you experience. In the 2004 introduction to *Jesus Calling* Sarah Young describes being in the presence of Jesus as feeling like there is a warm mist around her. In another part of the same introduction she says it is like having a bright light around her.

In addition, according to Jesus Calling there are numerous benefits that result from being in the presence of Jesus. For example, the presence of Jesus:

- helps you receive the peace of Jesus (October 13th)
- is a promise and a protection (October 15th)
- is a powerful protection and your best protection (October 15th)
- is the source of help (help flows from it) (October 16th)
- comforts you (October 16th)
- allows you to be a channel through whom others are comforted (October 16th)
- outshines any fantasy you can imagine (October 17th)
- enables you to face each day with confidence (October 18th)

My general impression is that, according to *Jesus Calling*, the presence of Jesus helps you relax, have peace, and to get through the day's troubles.

What do we need to do to experience the presence of Jesus?

Jesus Calling says that we are constantly in the presence of Jesus (Jan 28), and it seems to indicate that we can experience awareness of the presence of Jesus to greater and lesser degrees. How do we do this? The following are some of the instructions I found that seem to be related to becoming more aware of the presence of Jesus. These are from the 10th Anniversary Edition:

- Your weakness is the door to Jesus' presence (Jan 8)
- Ask Jesus to show you the path forward moment by moment (Jan 9)
- Make Jesus' presence the focal point of your thoughts (Jan 28)
- Whisper the name of Jesus (April 8)
- Thanksgiving and praise open the door to his presence (May 29)
- Attune yourself to Jesus' voice (September 26)

Jesus Calling gives many other ways to experience the presence of Jesus, but none of them are in accordance with scripture. So once again we have a complete disconnect with scripture.

Let me see if I can summarize the impressions I'm getting as I try to understand how to experience the presence of Jesus and its benefits according to *Jesus Calling*:

Jesus is a soft, fluffy, comfortable Jesus who is your best friend. He is always there to share the burden of your troubles, wipe away your tears, give you peace, and keep you feeling warm and comfortable inside. To experience the presence of Jesus you need to do things such as remember him, whisper his name, trust him, and turn to him when you are in need.

BUT... the problem is that this is not scriptural concerning coming into and being in the presence of Jesus, and this is not the Jesus of the Bible. This Jesus is not the Jesus who loves you, who truly cares about you, and who died for you.

What does scripture teach?

The healthy Christian is not necessarily the extrovert, ebullient Christian, but the Christian who has a sense of God's presence stamped deep on his soul, who trembles at God's word, who lets it dwell in him richly by constant meditation upon it, and who tests and reforms his life daily in response to it.
– J.I. Packer (http://tiny.cc/zqin5x)

What does it mean Biblically to be in the presence of God, and how do you Biblically come into the presence of God?

> *For thus says the high and exalted One Who lives forever, whose name is holy, "I dwell on a high and holy place, and also with the contrite and lowly of spirit"* – Isaiah 57:15

Consider this: Jesus is God and God is omnipresent. This means God is present everywhere at all times. That means everyone is always in the presence of God. It is impossible for us to move out of the presence of God.

But, this is not the type of presence we are referring to when we talk about Biblically being in the presence of Jesus. What it means is to be saved and thus be in a relationship with God. It is not a feeling or experience, as described in *Jesus Calling*. It is the reality of being seated with Christ in heaven the moment you are saved (Ephesians 2:6) It is the reality of having Christ dwell within you the moment you are saved (John 14:23 and 15:4).

It is true that at times we will feel distant from God. All Christians have experienced this. For example, after losing his wife to cancer C.S. Lewis wrote:

> *Why is He so present a commander in our time of prosperity and so very absent a help in time of trouble?* – C.S. Lewis, A Grief Observed, Chapter One, 1961

Peter explains what is happening:

> *In this you rejoice, though now for a little while, if necessary, you have been grieved by various trials, so that the tested genuineness of your faith—more precious than gold that perishes though it is tested by fire—may be found to result in praise and glory and honor at the revelation of Jesus Christ.* – 1 Peter 1:6-7 (ESV)

But, let's start at the beginning. How do we come into the presence of Jesus in the first place? What keeps us from the presence of God?

Fact #1 - Sin separates us from God.

But your iniquities have made a separation between you and your God, and your sins have hidden His face from you so that He does not hear. - Isaiah 59:2

Sin separates us from God. You are a sinner, and that means you are separated from God. His face is hidden from you. What can you do to change that? Nothing. Doing the things the Jesus in *Jesus Calling* commands you to do will not bring you any closer to Jesus. Sin is a barrier that cannot be breached by human effort.

We are born as sinners and that means we are natural enemies of God. But, the same verse that reveals we are enemies of God, also gives the solution:

For if, while we were enemies we were reconciled to God through the death of His Son, much more, having been reconciled, will we be saved by His life. - Romans 5:10

Fact #2 – We WERE enemies of God. But, we have been reconciled to God through the death of Jesus.

To be reconciled to God means we are no longer God's enemies, instead we are in a relationship with God. This happens through faith, which is a gift of God.

For you are saved by grace through faith, and this is not from yourselves; it is God's gift— not from works, so that no one can boast. - Ephesians 2:8-9

Through the faith given to you by God, you trust in the work of Jesus on the cross—His paying the penalty for your breaking God's laws—and you are saved from that penalty. Now, when God looks at you, instead of your sin He sees the righteousness of Jesus Christ. And that is why you, as a believer in the cross of Jesus Christ, are in a relationship with God.

If you have repented and are trusting that Christ has paid your penalty for sin... trusting that He paid your penalty for breaking God's laws... then you are free from the penalty for sin! Free from sin and united with Christ. AND Jesus is actually living in you now! Not only are you in the presence of Jesus, you have been united with

Jesus Christ your Lord.

> *I have been crucified with Christ; and it is no longer I who live, but Christ lives in me; and the life which I now live in the flesh I live by faith in the Son of God, who loved me and gave Himself up for me.* - Galatians 2:20

Jesus Calling constantly talks about being in the presence of Jesus, but never mentions sin, nor the cross, nor the gospel. *Jesus Calling* even tries to turn you away from being concerned about sin (Sept 7). BUT... without the cross we all are eternally separated from God. It is only through the cross that we enter the presence of God. Okay... I'm hearing some of you saying something again: *"Jesus Calling was written for Christians. Everyone who is reading it is already saved and is in a relationship with Jesus."*

Setting aside the question of whether or not everyone reading *Jesus Calling* is actually saved or not, this brings us to fact number three:

Fact #3 – All believers will experience the trial of feeling separated from God.

You are a believer, but you don't feel very close to God. What's wrong? John MacArthur explains:

> *A key passage in 1 Peter (1 Peter 1:3-7) will help you appreciate that times of distress are common and are for the good of God's children. Amid the rich details of God's glorious grace, resides an affirmation that those who rejoice in their salvation will also experience distress due to various trials.*

> *Take solace in knowing that sorrowful times--even periods of feeling God has withdrawn His presence--are an integral part of your spiritual experience. God hasn't utterly abandoned you, though you feel He has. Other believers have successfully traveled the dark path you walk and completed their journey.* – John McArthur, Why does God seem so distant when I need Him most? (http://tiny.cc/6lan5x)

When we are going through a time when we feel distant from God we can be encouraged that it is part of God's working to build our faith and growing us to know Him better. An article in the C.S. Lewis *Reflections* noted that:

Because C.S. Lewis did not give up, in time he was able to say, "I have gradually been coming to feel that the door is no longer shut and bolted." He came to see that God's silence during his grief was not a sign of indifference, cruelty, or abandonment. Rather, God had been at work for good in his life in ways he could not sense or imagine—bringing him into a deeper experience of the Lord than he had ever known before. – Reflections, C.S. Lewis Institute, July 2008

Based on 1 Peter 1:3-7 we can know that our time of darkness will be temporary, and that it has a purpose. It is a test of your faith that will strengthen your faith.

This sounds nothing at all like what *Jesus Calling* says. In *Jesus Calling* it is up to us to do something so we feel closer to Jesus. But, the reality is that God is in control. He does it all.

If I feel distant from Jesus, what should I do?

Be in prayer. Spend time talking with God. David's prayer in Psalm 13 is a good example.

Be in God's Word. Read your Bible every day and be in obedience to what you are reading. That is called seeking His righteousness. And remember, God is always present with you even when He feels far away (1 Peter 2:9). God is never far from a believer.

Examine yourself (2 Corinthians 13:5). Are you turning to sin for comfort instead of God? Or are you pure in heart (see Chapter 23)? The fact that sin separates you from God is foundational. You can't talk about being close to God without talking about sin, repentance, and confessing your sin to God. But, *Jesus Calling* says nothing about sin, repentance, redemption, nor confession of sin. It seems that *Jesus Calling* is about making you feel good, instead of being about the truth and leading you to a right relationship with God... which is the only way to have a close relationship with God.

And finally remember God is in control. These four points are not magic, meaning that if you do them you'll automatically feel closer to God. This is not the God of *Jesus Calling*. This is the true God, creator of you and the entire universe. God will draw nearer to you, when He determines the time is right.

CHAPTER 14
TRUSTING THE REAL JESUS

"EVERY TIME YOU AFFIRM YOUR TRUST IN ME, you put a coin into My treasury." - Jesus Calling January 10th, 10th Anniversary Edition, page 11 (capitalization as in the original).

"RELAX AND LET ME LEAD You through this day. I have everything under control." - Jesus Calling July 26th, 10th Anniversary Edition, page 217 (capitalization as in the original).

These quotes show two of the ways the "Jesus" of *Jesus Calling* tells you to trust him. In the first you are to affirm "your trust" (whatever that means). In the other, although it does not specifically mention the word "trust," you are commanded to relax and trust Jesus to lead you through the day.

The Bible also tells us to trust Jesus. But... and this is important... in a very different way. The key question we'll look at in this chapter is: what are we to trust Jesus for?

Trusting the Jesus of *Jesus Calling*

Once again I picked a random date. Then I looked at the next ten days of devotions and wrote down the benefits *Jesus Calling* seems to identify as a result of trusting Jesus. Remember, although I tried to stay with a literal reading, it is easy to interpret *Jesus Calling* in many different ways. So if you repeat what I've done, you may get a slightly different result.

Here is the list of the benefits of trusting Jesus, based on ten days in February. According to *Jesus Calling* you are to trust Jesus to:

- get you safely through the day (February 3rd)
- guide you through the day (February 4th)
- give you peace (February 5th)
- give you rest (February 6th)
- guide you through the day (February 7th)
- help you deal with your problems (February 8th)
- be your Strength and Song (February 9th)
- bend time and events in your favor (February 10th)
- train you (February 11th)
- be near you (February 12th)

To summarize the above, I'd say that Jesus wants us to have a good day. If you trust him, he'll guide you through the day, keeping you safe, eliminating troubles, and giving you strength and peace. My impression from reading numerous *Jesus Calling* devotions is that to trust means to stop trying to figure out what to do…. whatever will be, will be. Trust Jesus to guide you and deal with whatever comes up, and you will have peace.

And as you read *Jesus* Calling, you find that these benefits depend on what you do and how well you trust Jesus. As your level of trust varies, so will Jesus' response and the resulting benefits. As we'll see in a few minutes, that's nothing like trusting the Jesus of the Bible!

BUT FIRST: What's this about bending time and events in your favor?

I find February 10th (in the above list) to be particularly self-focused and disturbing. If Jesus is bending time and events in my favor, what impact does that have on everyone else?

Back in the old days, before I was saved and when I had to commute through city traffic, I'd think about traffic lights. Wouldn't it be great if God favored me with all green lights? But, if God favors me this way, what about the people that needed to cross my path? They get caught at red lights because God is giving me all green lights. God's favor on me results in other people being delayed and inconvenienced. Am I really that special? I don't think so.

Besides what was the real problem? It was not traffic and getting stopped by red lights. The problem was that I wanted to be god, doing whatever I wanted, and having my path cleared so I would not be inconvenienced. The problem was my self-centeredness. I wanted to make everyone get out of my way so I could get to where I wanted to be quickly. But, God is not a genie who makes my life easier and the consequences of my bad decisions go away. God does not bent time and events to favor me.

Trusting the Jesus of the Bible

Trust in the LORD *with all your heart, and do not lean on your own understanding.* - Proverbs 3:5

What does it mean to trust the Jesus of the Bible? It means you can trust His character. You can trust His wisdom, His power, His faithfulness, and His goodness. And that means you can trust His promises. For example, Jesus has promised that if you believe in Him, you will not perish:

For God so loved the world, that He gave His only begotten Son, that whoever believes in Him shall not perish, but have eternal life. - John 3:16

This is a promise of salvation. Believers are promised eternal life. Jesus is saying that if you trust Him, you will not experience the second death—the lake of fire—but will experience eternal life in God's presence in heaven forever. What a wonderful promise!

What is the source of Biblical trust?

"Trusting is what we do because of the faith we have been given. Trusting is believing in the promises of God in all circumstances, even in those where the evidence seems to be to the contrary." – Got Questions Ministries, (http://tiny.cc/0avz4x)

We trust God as a result of the faith He has given us, a faith the results in salvation. God gives us faith, and as a result of that faith we trust in what Jesus did on the cross. And we also trust God's other promises.

What are some of God's promises?

God has promised us many things. The beginning of everything is His promise of salvation. If you are not trusting in His promise of salvation, you do not have any of His other promises:

> *And this is the promise that he made to us—eternal life.* - 1 John 2:25 (ESV)

And He promises that the work of growing you to become like Jesus, that He began in you at salvation, will be completed:

> *For I am confident of this very thing, that He* [God] *who began a good work in you will perfect it until the day of Christ Jesus.* - Philippians 1:6

Let's look at some of the other promises God gives in the scripture references used in *Jesus Calling*. In doing this I am making the assumption that the scripture references are supposed to be related to what is said on their associated devotion page. Let's start with Jesus' promise of rest:

> *"Come to Me, all who are weary and heavy-laden, and I will give you rest. Take My yoke upon you and learn from Me, for I am gentle and humble in heart, and* YOU WILL FIND REST FOR YOUR SOULS. *For My yoke is easy and My burden is light."* - Matthew 11:28-31

Ahhh... this sounds good. You've had a hard day at work and Jesus promises you rest. You don't need to be concerned about what needs to be done next. Let your spirit rest. That is a description of the rest *Jesus Calling* promises. Physical rest. Rest from worrying about the future. It sounds wonderful. Let's look at two of the devotions that reference Matthew 11:28:

- *Jesus Calling* for June 27th promises that you can rest with Jesus

78

after a hard day, trusting that he will equip you for everything you need to do.

- *Jesus Calling* for February 25th promises that you can rest in the presence of Jesus while He guides you through the day.

The problem is, this is not the rest the Jesus of the Bible promises. Matthew 11:28-31 is talking about sin. Jesus is saying that if you submit to Him and come to Him for salvation, and you will receive rest from carrying the heavy burden of sin and doing the heavy work of trying to please God. John MacArthur explains this verse:

> *"To come is to believe to the point of submitting to His lordship."* - John MacArthur New Testament Commentary Matthew 8-15, 1987, page 274

> *"Jesus gives a call to repent, to turn away from the self-centered and works-center life and come to Him. The person who is weary and heavy-laden despairs of his own ability to please God. He comes to the end of his own resources and turns to Christ."* - John MacArthur New Testament Commentary Matthew 8-15, 1987, page 274

Jesus' greatest concern is about sin and your salvation from the eternal consequences for sin. Jesus loves you. He loves you so much that He suffered and died for you... so that you may live... free from the heavy burden of sin and worthless efforts to save yourself. That is the rest Jesus is talking about. As is typical, *Jesus Calling* has totally missed the mark.

Let's look at another verse. In Philippians Jesus promises us peace.

> *Be anxious for nothing, but in everything by prayer and supplication with thanksgiving let your requests be made known to God. And the peace of God, which surpasses all comprehension, will guard your hearts and your minds in Christ Jesus.* - Philippians 4:6-7

Now let's look at two *Jesus Calling* devotions that reference these verses. Here are my paraphrases:

- *Jesus Calling* for January 15th promises you peace, if you focus on Jesus... focus your eyes on Jesus instead of focusing on your daily problems.

- *Jesus Calling* for March 1st tells you that Jesus promises you perfect peace, as long as you have a well-developed trust in Jesus. It is not clear, but it appears you need to intentionally act to trust Jesus to help you to get through your daily troubles.

Again, neither one of these reflect what the referenced scripture is actually teaching. In *Jesus Calling* you are promised peace, if you do something, such as trusting Jesus to deal with your problems and troubles.

However, Philippians 4:6-7 is not a promise of future peace. It does not say you will have peace. It is a statement about the reality of the peace you already have. As a believer you received peace the day you were saved. It is one of the fruits of the Spirit, and it is not a peace that results from anything you do. It is the peace that comes from being at peace with God.

> *"This peace is for those who are already at peace with God through justification by faith in Jesus Christ.... For the peace of God not only suffices but far surpasses human comprehension. It acts as a sentry to guard the believer's heart and the believer's thoughts from all anxiety and despair."* - Homer Kent Jr., The Expositor's Bible Commentary, 1978, page 152

Jesus Calling once again gets things backward. It's not that, if you trust Jesus to take away anxiety and troubles, you will then have peace. What scripture says is that as a believer you already have peace, and it is this already existing peace that will take away your anxiety and despair.

It is particularly troubling that the March 1st *Jesus Calling* devotion makes peace conditional... you'll have peace as long as you have a well-developed trust (whatever that is). Other *Jesus Calling* devotions say Jesus will give his promised peace to the extent you are trusting him. This implies your trust in Jesus can vary, and if you stop trusting in Jesus you lose the peace that comes from Jesus.

A theme of *Jesus Calling* that, if you do the right things, you can get from Jesus what you need to make your daily life more relaxing and peaceful. If you trust him, he will take away anxiety and give you good stuff like peace. The trust comes from you, and the better you do at giving trust to Jesus, the more peace you receive in return. That is the description of a New Age pagan type of god. It IS NOT the God of the Bible.

Scripture shows us that trust comes from our faith, and faith is a gift from God.

> *For by grace you have been saved through faith; and that not of yourselves, it is the gift of God; not as a result of works, so that no one may boast.* - Ephesians 2:8-9

When we are saved we receive peace, along with the other fruits of the Spirit.

> *But the fruit of the Spirit is love, joy, peace, patience, kindness, goodness, faithfulness, gentleness, self-control; against such things there is no law.* - Galatians 5:22-23

However, it is possible to quench the Spirit through sin, and then have some of the fruits of the spirit to a lesser degree than you should have. In other words, you many not experience the full peace of the Holy Spirit, because you have unconfessed sin in your life. Again we see that *Jesus Calling* totally misses the point—the problem is sin. Unless we deal with sin, none of our other problems or troubles will ever be solved.

How to get rid of anxiety and fear – the Biblical answer

Jesus Calling talks a lot about eliminating anxiety through trusting Jesus. However, scripture tells us that we need not worry or have anxiety about tomorrow, because we already know God will finish the work He has begun in us. This means, in part, that God will provide what we need. He can't finish His work in us, unless He provides what we need each day. So we know He will provide all that we need. For example:

This is why I tell you: Don't worry about your life, what you will eat or what you will drink; or about your body, what you will wear.
– Matthew 6:25

In *Jesus Calling* we are to not to dwell on the future, but focus on the present. Jesus will deal with the future, if we are trusting him. The stronger our trust, the more Jesus provides. Then we will have peace.

By the way, did you notice that this puts you in control of God? If you trust, then He responds by handling your problems—and that is why you don't need to be concerned about the future. This is similar to the pagan gods of Jesus' day, and the promises of the Hindu gods of today. You do things for them, and in return they may give you what you want. The only problem is, like the Jesus of *Jesus Calling*, they are not real.

Scripture says that we trust God because of the faith He has given us. Why do we not need to be anxious? Because the peace of God, that we already have, brings contentment. No matter what our circumstances, whether we are freezing and starving, or living in luxury, we know God is in control. Whether we face health problems and constant troubles every day, or have a great job and a trouble-free life, God is in control. Even our trust is a gift from God. He gives us faith and our trust comes from that faith. Everything comes from God and we are content.

If we are submitted to Him, living in His word and obeying Him, His will is being done. That is a different trust than the trust of *Jesus Calling*.

I have learned to be content in whatever circumstances I am. I know both how to have a little, and I know how to have a lot. In any and all circumstances I have learned the secret of being content—whether well fed or hungry, whether in abundance or in need. I am able to do all things through Him who strengthens me. - Philippians 4:11b-13

When it comes to trusting Jesus, trust the Jesus of the Bible.

> If you are experiencing fear or anxiety, please see Chapter 8 for information about getting help from a Christian counselor.

CHAPTER 15
WHAT IS THE PEACE OF GOD?

Jesus Calling
Enjoying Peace in His Presence

Let's talk about peace. To do that we'll first need to talk about false teaching. False teaching is frequently very close to Biblical teaching, and we need to be able to discern the difference. That means being able to distinguish the right from the almost right... to be able to see the counterfeit that is so very close to the truth. In addition, in many cases, such as what we'll see here, it's not just having the ability to see what is wrong, but also to notice what you don't see. With the topic of peace we'll see how false teaching can look very good, but in many cases the truth just camouflages the false teaching.

For example, here are some quotes about peace from *Jesus Calling*. These come from the 10th Anniversary Edition, published in 2014. Peace is a common theme throughout *Jesus Calling*, so to narrow things down I looked for quotes from days for which Philippians 4:6-7 was one of the referenced scriptures. We'll see why in a few moments. Capitalization is as it is in the original.

"To provide this radiant Peace for you, I died a criminal's death." – February 13

"WHEN SOMETHING IN YOUR LIFE OR THOUGHTS

makes you anxious, come to Me and talk about it, Bring Me your prayer and petition with thanksgiving, saying "Thank you Jesus for this opportunity to trust You more." – March 1st

"PEACE IS MY CONTINUAL GIFT TO YOU. It flows abundantly from My throne of Grace." – April 18th

These quotes sound good. They seem to be Biblical. So… you can be reading your daily devotion in *Jesus Calling* and it will sound Biblical. (If you've already spotted a problem, please hold those thoughts for a minute.)

Now let's take a look at a quote about peace from John MacArthur. This comes from a booklet I highly recommend, *"Found: God's Peace, Experience True Freedom From Anxiety In Every Circumstance."* If I could, I'd just reproduce this short booklet here, as it thoroughly addresses the topic of Biblical peace. If you'd like to read it, copies may be purchased on the Grace To You web site (www.GTY.org) for just $2.00, and that includes shipping. (http://tiny.cc/wot84x)

"We allow our daily concerns to turn into worry and therefore sin when our thoughts become focused on changing the future instead of doing our best to handle our present circumstances. Such thoughts are unproductive. They end up controlling us—though it should be the other way around—and cause us to neglect other responsibilities and relationships. If we don't deal with those feelings in a productive manner by getting back on track in life, we'll lose hope instead of finding answers. When left unresolved, worry can debilitate one's mind and body—and even lead to panic attacks." – John MacArthur, Found: God's Peace, Experience True Freedom From Anxiety In Every Circumstance, 2015 – Introduction, Kindle version location 27 of 703

This sounds like something you'd read in *Jesus Calling*. So it looks like there are no problems. John MacArthur and Sarah Young are in agreement when it comes to peace. Well… hold on… let's not jump to conclusions. Let's add just a little more background.

How can you identify false teaching? What do you look for?

According to John MacArthur, a characteristic of false teaching is that the emphasis is in the wrong place. Instead of being focused on Jesus (the true Jesus), the gospel, and glorifying God, the emphasis is on feelings, experiences, prophecy, blessings, healings, angels, or miracles. You typically won't see all of these in one false teacher, but you will always see several of them, if you look deep enough. The general principle is that false teaching frequently focuses on the by-products of the faith instead of on faith. It focuses more on what you can get, instead of the gospel and the glory of God.

We see that in *Jesus Calling*. It promises that you will get rid of your fears, anxiety, worry and lack of peace... but you do it through your own efforts... for example, by focusing just on the present and putting thoughts about the future out of your mind. That's not what the Bible says. So, let's start by learning the Biblical solution to experiencing fear, anxiety, worry, and a lack of peace.

The Biblical solution - Philippians 4:6-9

For every problem mentioned in the Bible, scripture has a solution. Philippians 4:6-9 gives us the solution for anxiety and worry. That's why I looked for *Jesus Calling* devotions that included Philippians 4 as a referenced scripture. Here's what it says:

> *Be anxious for nothing, but in everything by prayer and supplication with thanksgiving let your requests be made known to God. And the peace of God, which surpasses all comprehension, will guard your hearts and your minds in Christ Jesus.*
>
> *Finally, brethren, whatever is true, whatever is honorable, whatever is right, whatever is pure, whatever is lovely, whatever is of good repute, if there is any excellence and if anything worthy of praise, dwell on these things. The things you have learned and received and heard and seen in me, practice these things, and the God of peace will be with you.* - Philippians 4:6-9

What are we to do? Philippians tell us to do three things. John MacArthur, in *"Found: God's Peace,"* summarizes them as:

1. Right Prayer
2. Right Thinking
3. Right Action

What is right prayer?

Right prayer is thankful prayer, realizing that God's promises are sure. One of those promises is peace: Philippians 4:7—*the peace of God, which surpasses all comprehension, will guard your hearts and your minds in Christ Jesus.*

Right prayer comes from being content, whatever your circumstances. Right prayer means being thankful, whatever your circumstances. When Jonah was swallowed by a great fish, what did he pray? A prayer of thanks (Jonah 2). When I try to imagine being swallowed by a fish, I have trouble bringing up thoughts of thankfulness. But Jonah was praising the Lord from the inside of the belly of a great fish. That is right prayer.

We pray with thankfulness, recognizing that God causes all things to work together for good to those who love God (Romans 8:28); and that God will perfect, confirm, strengthen and establish you, although sometimes you may first suffer a little (1 Peter 5:10); and that God will not allow you to be tempted beyond what you are able to endure (1 Corinthians 10:13). Remember God's promises and pray with thanksgiving!

What is right thinking?

Right thinking means to fill our thoughts with *whatever is true, whatever is honorable, whatever is right, whatever is pure, whatever is lovely, whatever is of good repute.* A good place to start is to fill our thoughts with scripture. This is one of the reasons why memorizing scripture is so useful. When you face troubles, you can recall memorized scripture.

Set your mind on the things above, not on the things that are on earth.
– Colossians 3:2

In addition to scripture, some human activities also fit in the categories Paul lists. Recall memories of whatever is true, honorable, right, pure, lovely, and of good repute, keeping in mind that it is God who defines these terms, not man. In his helpful pamphlet about fear Jay Adams writes:

86

What Do You Do When

FEAR

Overcomes You?

JAY E. ADAMS

"Whenever you catch your mind wandering back into the forbidden territory (and you can be sure it will—more frequently early on, until you retrain and discipline it to love), change the direction of your thought. Do not allow yourself one conscious moment of such thought. Instead, quickly ask God to help you refocus upon those things that fit into Paul's listed recorded in Philippians 4:8-9. The attitude must grow within you that says, "So if I have a fear experience, so what? It's unpleasant, it's disturbing, but I'll live through it—at least I always have before." When you can honestly think this way without becoming anxious, you will know that the change has been made." —

Jay Adams, What Do You Do When Fear Overcomes You, 1975, P&R Publishing

The principle he is talking about is given in Proverbs 23:7 -- *For as he thinks within himself, so he is.*

What is right action?

I grew up in a church that preached from the pulpit that we should feed the hungry, visit the prisons, and help those who are poor. But when everyone went home, nothing happened. When I went off to college I stopped going to church—they are nothing but hypocrites. Philippians says: *the things you have learned and received and heard and seen in me, practice these things.*

If we don't practice what we preach, we are hypocrites. Our Godly thoughts and attitudes must express themselves in Godly actions. What should we be doing? The New Testament shows us how we should live. Right action is not just helping other people, it involves living according to God's commandments. It means being honest and trustworthy, it means loving your neighbor (even if you don't like them), and it means being kind in your speech and generous in actions. This type of behavior doesn't just happen. Just as an athlete trains to win the game, you need to train yourself to do good.

If you want to eliminate anxiety and worries, that's what scripture says to do. Be in right prayer; have right thinking; and do right actions. How does this compare with *Jesus Calling?* Let's take a look at a few more quotes from the 10th Anniversary Edition of *Jesus Calling*, 2014.

> *"PEACE BE WITH YOU! Ever since the resurrection this has been My watchword to those who yearn for Me. As you sit quietly, let My Peace settle over you and enfold you in My Loving Presence. To provide this radiant Peace for you, I died a criminal's death. Receive My peace abundantly and thankfully."* – February 13th

1. Right Prayer

2. Right Thinking

3. Right Action

This gives the context of the February 13th quote given at the beginning of this chapter. It even mentions the cross. But, do you see it? Do you see what is missing?

A common tactic used by magicians is to distract you away from what they don't want you to see. They may draw your attention to what they are doing with their right hand, while using their left hand to accomplish the "magic." The same approach can be used in false teaching.

Jesus Calling tells you to pray with thanksgiving. That's good. False teaching never has a problem encouraging people to pray. Praying to a false god has no power. So it is common to see praying accompanying false teaching, and to see false teaching urging you to pray. It's a Biblical truth that can be used to direct your attention away from the false teaching.

What about the gospel? The cross is mentioned in this quote… or is it? Let's go through this slowly, because we are going to see a false gospel.

What does this quote say about the death of Jesus? He died a criminal's death. That's true, but does it have anything of the gospel in it? Or are you reading your Biblical knowledge into this statement?

Ted Bundy died a criminal's death, executed in the electric chair in Florida. He was a serial killer who brutally murdered 30 women. Apparently he was the same as Jesus… he died a criminal's death.

What did Jesus actually do to provide peace for you? It wasn't because he died a criminal's death. It was because He died, and took the full wrath of God on Himself, to pay the penalty you've earned as a result of breaking God's laws. Jesus' substitutionary death on the cross provides God's salvation and peace. You won't read about that anywhere in *Jesus Calling*. Saying that you have peace because Christ died a criminal's death is a false gospel.

What else is missing?

I'm hearing some of you saying, *"You can't look at just three, short devotions and expect to find a complete description of how we receive God's peace."* Okay, let's add two more, again from the 10th Anniversary Edition of *Jesus Calling* (2014)

> *"The best way to receive this gift* [peace] *is to sit quietly in My presence, trusting Me in every area of your life. Quietness and trust accomplish far more than you can imagine: not only in you, but also on earth and in heaven."* – September 12th

> *"Thank Me for My peaceful Presence, regardless of your feelings. Whisper My Name in loving tenderness. My Peace, which lives continually in your spirit, will gradually work its way through your entire being."* – December 31st

The five quotes given in this chapter are representative of what the rest of *Jesus Calling* says about peace. It is exactly as I have been describing, and it is not Biblical.

The lie of omission. What is missing?

There is no mention of filling your thoughts with what is good and right, as commanded in scripture. Instead, what is commanded by the "Jesus" of *Jesus Calling* is the New Age practice of sitting in stillness and quietly repeating a single word... in this case the word "Jesus." (*"Whisper my name..."*)

There is no mention of putting right thinking into action... or doing right actions. Instead you are commanded to sit quietly and essentially do nothing, except whisper the name of Jesus over and over. That's not scriptural.

What is missing is most of Philippians 4:6-9. *Jesus Calling* uses Biblical sounding language, but replaces what the scripture teaches with New Age "spiritual" practices. It may sound "good," but it is not Biblical.

What does Jesus Calling say to do?

I made a list of what these quotes from *Jesus Calling* say you should do:

- Sit quietly
- Let My peace flow over you
- Trust Me in every area of your life
- Thank Me for My peaceful presence
- Come to Me, talk to Me
- Pray "Thank you Jesus."
- Whisper the name of Jesus over and over.

The September 12th devotion summarizes it: *"Quietness and trust accomplish far more than you can imagine: not only in you, but also on earth and in heaven."*

Does any of this sound at all like what scripture says? No. While it may sound good when you are reading it, it does not stand up to being compared with scripture. Sitting quietly, whispering Jesus' name, and letting peace flow over you is not Biblical. It is a New Age spiritual practice.

The "peace" of *Jesus Calling* IS NOT THE PEACE of the TRUE JESUS CHRIST, OUR LORD and SAVIOR.

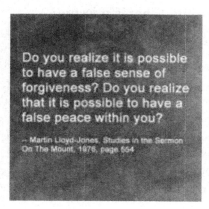

Do you realize it is possible to have a false sense of forgiveness? Do you realize that it is possible to have a false peace within you?

-- Martin Lloyd-Jones, *Studies in the Sermon On The Mount*, 1976, page 554

CHAPTER 16
FINDING REAL PEACE

"Peace flows from sanctification, but they being unregenerate, have nothing to do with peace. 'There is no peace, saith my God to the wicked.' Isa 57: 21. They may have a truce, but no peace. God may forbear the wicked a while, and stop the roaring of his cannon; but though there be a truce, yet there is no peace. The wicked may have something which looks like peace, but it is not. They may be fearless and stupid; but there is a great difference between a stupified conscience, and a pacified conscience. 'When a strong man armed keepeth his palace, his goods are in peace.' Luke 11: 21. This is the devil's peace; he rocks men in the cradle of security; he cries, Peace, peace, when men are on the precipice of hell. The seeming peace a sinner has, is not from the knowledge of his happiness, but the ignorance of his danger." – Thomas Watson, A Body of Divinity, http://tiny.cc/c85c5x

The natural man, that's us as we are from birth, is at war with God. It may not feel like it. Before you were saved you may have felt very spiritual. You may have felt like you had a close relationship with god. But, it was something else you were close to, not the God of the Bible. As I mentioned in a previous chapter, we are born enemies of God and we need to be reconciled with God:

> *For if while we were enemies we were reconciled to God through the death of His Son, much more, having been reconciled, we shall be saved by His life.*
> – Romans 5:10

It is only when we are reconciled with God... meaning we are at

91

peace with God... that we come into His presence. Remember, sin separates us from God. Until we are washed free from sin, there is a wall between us and God. In reality it all happens in the blink of an eye. When we trust in Jesus as our savior, the barrier created by sin is gone, and we immediately have peace and are in the presence of God.

> *...even when we were dead in our transgressions, [God] made us alive together with Christ (by grace you have been saved), and raised us up with Him, and seated us with Him in the heavenly places in Christ Jesus,* - Ephesians 2:5-6

Added to peace, being together with Christ, and being seated with Christ in the heavenly places, once we are at peace with God, we are immediately blessed with EVERY spiritual blessing. Every one!

> *Blessed be the God and Father of our Lord Jesus Christ, who has blessed us with every spiritual blessing in the heavenly places in Christ,* – Ephesian 1:3

That's right! As believers we are there now, seated with Him. And we have been blessed with every spiritual blessing. Look at the wording in Ephesians 2:5-6 and 1:3. It's not in the future. We have been seated (past tense) with Him and He has blessed (past tense) us. When you trust Jesus as your savior, you are at peace and you are seated with Him, and blessed by Him, That's far better than what *Jesus Calling* promises.

But not only that, we are united with Christ. Jesus Christ is living in all believers, right now. You can't get any closer to Jesus than that.

> *Do you not recognize this about yourselves, that Jesus Christ is in you.* – 2 Corinthians 13:5

> *I have been crucified with Christ; and it is no longer I who live, but Christ lives in me;* - Galatians 2:20

All of this... being seated with Him, being blessed with every spiritual blessing, and having Christ living in you... results from being reconciled to God... from being at peace with God. And that results from trusting Jesus as your savior. That is real peace.

How can you be reconciled with God?

If you are going to solve a problem, you first need to recognize there is a problem. So what is the problem we all have? Sin. Sin keeps us separated from God. Sin keeps us out of the presence of God. And as long as you are an unrepentant sinner, you cannot come into the presence of Jesus.

What is sin?

Sin is thinking and behaving in a way that is not characteristic of God. The Ten Commandments, for example, describe the character of God and what we should be like. When we obey the Ten Commandments, we are behaving in accordance with the character of God. When we break God's law... meaning, for example, we disobey one of the Ten Commandments, we are acting contrary to God's character.

But, no one can live perfectly!! No one can perfectly obey all of the Ten Commandments all of the time! That's true, it's impossible. Yet that is what God requires. If you do not perfectly obey all of the Ten Commandments, every day, every minute, then your destiny is the lake of fire... hell... for eternity (that's forever and ever with no end).

But, Jesus loves you and He provided the answer:

2000 years ago Jesus died on the cross paying the penalty for every one of God's laws you've broken. He offers the cross to you as a free gift. If you accept it, if you repent (turn away from breaking God's laws and toward obeying God) and  trust that Jesus truly paid your penalty in full, then your sins are forgiven... they are totally washed away by the blood of Jesus. If you trust in Jesus as your savior, sin no longer separates you from God! Praise God for His love, mercy and grace that gave you this free gift!

And you were dead in your trespasses and sins, in which you formerly walked according to the course of this world, according to the prince of the power of the air, of the spirit that is now working in the sons of disobedience. Among them we too all formerly lived in the lusts of our flesh, indulging the desires of the flesh and of the mind, and were by nature children of wrath, even as the rest. But God, being rich in mercy, because of His great love with which He loved us, even when we were dead in transgressions, made us alive together with Christ (by grace you have been saved), and raised us up with Him, and seated us with Him in the heavenly places in Christ Jesus, so that in the ages to come He might show the surpassing riches of His grace in kindness toward us in Christ Jesus. For by grace you have been saved through faith; and that not of yourselves; it is the gift of God, not as a result of works, so that no one can boast. - Ephesians 2:1-9

Jesus Calling almost talks about this in the July 3th devotion. It says that:

"I have acquitted you through My own blood. Your acquittal came at the price of My unparalleled sacrifice." – Jesus Calling, 10th Anniversary Edition, 2014, July 3rd, page 194

The book you are reading could have been just one page. All I needed to do is give the above quote and *Jesus Calling* is instantly revealed as false teaching and a false gospel. Preaching a false gospel is a sure Biblical sign of a false teacher. And scripture tells us to run from false teachers, don't let them in your home!

Let me take a moment to explain why I say the July 3rd devotion is a false gospel. The quote from *Jesus Calling* says, *I have acquitted you through my blood..."* What does acquit mean? The dictionary definition is:

free (someone) from a criminal charge by a verdict of not guilty – The Oxford Dictionary of English

To acquit someone means they have been declared innocent. They did not commit the crime. Acquittal means they did nothing wrong. Think about it. If you've been acquitted—declared innocent—why did Jesus die on the cross? Was it just for fun? If you are innocent, then Jesus does not need to die to pay your penalty for sin. There is no penalty. Since God's judgment is always true, to be acquitted means you have never broken any of God's laws. You are innocent! But, that's not what scripture says:

But, that's not our situation. You are guilty, there is no question about it. Even your conscience testifies that you have broken God's laws. You know you have earned the just penalty for breaking God's laws. And the judge, God, knows all the evidence. He knows your every thought. His judgment is true, correct, and just. You are guilty.

If we say that we have no sin, we are deceiving ourselves and the truth is not in us. – 1 John 1:8

In fact, if you have broken just one of God's laws, you are guilty of breaking them all:

For whoever keeps the whole law and yet stumbles in one point, he has become guilty of all. – James 2:10

Now let's learn what really happened… you are guilty. You have broken God's laws. You are standing before the judge and the verdict is guilty… the penalty is death. Then Jesus steps up and says, *"I'll pay the penalty for this person."* And Jesus pays the penalty you've earned for sin in full. That's why scripture never uses the word "acquit" but refers to this as "redeemed." You have been redeemed by Christ. He paid the price to free you from sin. If you accept this free gift, it is yours.

That is not the message of *Jesus Calling*… yet this is the message Jesus desperately wants you to know. This is the gospel. It is Jesus Christ calling you to a new life through the cross. Calling you to be born again. Jesus died, was buried, and on the third day rose from the dead, demonstrating to all who will listen, there IS life after death!

That truly IS good news. And Jesus is calling you to hear this good news, and accept it as true. Will you do that right now?

In the July 3rd devotion Jesus preaches a false gospel. That is a FALSE JESUS and a FALSE GOSPEL. **RUN! From *Jesus Calling.***

In chapter one I asked you to fill-in-the-blank with what you'd call putting words in the mouth of Jesus. Now that you've seen some of the results of putting words in the mouth of Jesus, answer this question again:

Do you think this book has been too harsh? When God is represented as having said something He never said, what would you call that? (Write your answer here: _____.)

Has your answer changed? Why?

If you'd like to share your story about *Jesus Calling*, or how this book (the one you are reading now) has impacted your life, please send me an email. I'd love to hear your story. I can't promise I'll be able to answer every email, but I will read them all—if you keep it short. My email address is:

ChristsLove4You@gmail.com

I hope to put the answers to common questions I receive on my web site at: www.NotJesusCalling.com. By sending me an email you give me permission to quote that email on the web site, in a future book, or in a future article. BTW, I have no budget for building a web site, so please be patient it may take some time.

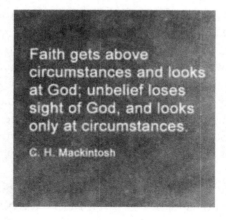

Faith gets above circumstances and looks at God; unbelief loses sight of God, and looks only at circumstances.

C. H. Mackintosh

PART III – WHAT DOES JESUS ACTUALLY SAY?

CHAPTER 17
BECOMING LIKE JESUS

What goal do we have for ourselves as Christians? The goal of all Christians is to become like Jesus... to have the character of Jesus. Not only is that our goal, it is also God's goal. He has predestined all believers to be conformed to the likeness of His Son (Romans 8:29). And God will see that work through until it is finished (Philippians 1:6).

If you could pick one word to describe Christ, what would it be? Love. If we are to become like Christ, we need to learn how to love like Jesus. So, what is Biblical love?

What is Biblical love? How do we love like Jesus?

Love is patient, love is kind and is not jealous; love does not brag and is not arrogant, does not act unbecomingly; it does not seek its own, is not provoked, does not take into account a wrong suffered, does not rejoice in unrighteousness, but rejoices with the truth; bears all things, believes all things, hopes all things, endures all things. – 1 Corinthians 13:4-7.

When someone says "love" we think of romantic love. We can fall in love in an instant. But, the downside is that we can also fall out of love in an instant. Love can be won and love can be lost. But, none of this is characteristic of the way Jesus loves you.

97

The Greek word most commonly translated as "love" is agape. When 1 John 4:8 says *"God is love."* John is saying *"God is agape."* Romans 5:8 says, *"But God demonstrates His own love*—or if we don't translate the word agape— *God demonstrated His own agape toward us, in that while we were yet sinners, Christ died for us."*

What is this agape? It is the word that describes the way Christ loves us. It is the word that describes how we should love God and love others.

Agape is not a feeling

Biblical love is not a feeling. Biblical love is an attitude that results in action. You DO love. How do you do love? You do it with patience and without jealousy or bragging about what you are doing. You do love by not being arrogant, by not seeking to serve yourself, and by being polite and respectful of others. You do love by not taking into account wrongs done against you, nor do you rejoice in unrighteousness (sin), but instead you rejoice in truth. And that's just the beginning.

To summarize it briefly, agape means to have an attitude of sacrificially giving of yourself to help others with their true needs. It does not mean giving just because someone asks for something. It is giving to help others with their true needs.

So when Jesus says we are to love our enemies (Matthew 5:44), that does not mean we are to love them emotionally. We don't even need to like them. But, we are commanded to sacrificially help them with their true needs. If someone we dislike needs a drink of water, we give them a cup of cool, clean water.

John 3:16 is one of the best known verses in the Bible, and it talks about God's love for us. He gave us the one thing we most needed, He saved us from the eternal death of hell:

> *For God so loved the world, that he gave his only Son, that whoever believes in him should not perish but have eternal life.* – John 3:16

We commonly read this verse as, "God liked us so much, that He gave His only Son..." But, is that what it means? No... not at all.

I like the footnote you'll find in the ESV Bible. It provides an alternate translation for the first part of John 3:16. Instead of "For

God so loved the world..." the alternate translation says:

> *For this is how God loved the world,* -- this is the action God did -- *that he gave his only Son, that whoever believes in him should not perish but have eternal life.* – John 3:16 (ESV)

"For this is how God loved the world..." Biblical love is an action, and John 3:16 describes the action God took. The Son of God, Jesus Christ, died on the cross to pay the penalty you've earned for breaking God's laws. That is how God loved you. God didn't love you just with His words. God didn't love you just with His feelings. He loved you with His actions, and because of that He saved you from the penalty you've earned for disobeying God. Praise God, and THANK YOU LORD!!

For this is how
God loved the world,
that he gave his only Son,
that whoever believes
in him should not perish
but have eternal life.
– John 3:16 (ESV)

How do we love God?

Jesus describes agape love and the actions of obeying His commands as being the same:

> *"If you love Me, you will keep My commandments."* - John 14:15

When you obey Jesus' commands, what are you doing? You are acting in accordance with the character of God. You are doing what God would do. How do you know what God would do? Scripture has given you His commandments, sometimes called God's laws. His laws describe His character, and when you obey God's laws you are conforming yourself to God's character.

> *He who has My commandments and keeps them is the one who loves Me;* – John 14:21

Jesus repeats this statement over and over. When Jesus repeats something, you know it is important, pay attention. When He repeats it multiple times, it is extremely important. PAY ATTENTION!

If anyone loves Me, he will keep My word; – John 14:23

And this is love, that we walk according to His commandments.
- 2 John 6

Biblically, loving God is an action of obedience to God's commands. If you are loving Christ, you will be doing those actions He has commanded you to do. If you doing those things Christ, in scripture, has told you to do, then you are loving God.

What has Christ commanded all of us to do? In asking this question we are getting to the heart of one of the major problems with *Jesus Calling.*

Jesus Calling is a devotional book that is packed with commands from Jesus. It straight out tells you what to do and not do... how to live your life... and the attitude about life you should have. *Jesus Calling* is packed with commands from "Jesus." But, what the "Jesus" of *Jesus Calling* commands is, in many cases, very different from what scripture commands.

My summary of the most frequently expressed command in *Jesus Calling* would be—sit quietly, just relax...don't do much planning for the future...don't be concerned about your troubles... let Jesus take care of everything. Relax and feel the warm mist of Jesus enveloping you.

Is this what Jesus wants you to do? No!

What would a "to-do" list from the real Jesus look like? Let's go right to the top of the list. What was the most important item on Jesus' to-do list? What is so important that Jesus was willing to die so that it could be accomplished? Jesus answers this question in scripture. It is the main story that runs throughout the Bible, from Genesis 3 to Revelation 22.

The answer: it is the story of restoration. Jesus wants all of us to be restored to the perfect condition in which we were originally created. Do you know the story? Here is what happened:

Mankind was originally created in the image of God (Genesis 1). The fall (Genesis 3) destroyed that image and brought sin into the world. Since that time every human has been born with a sin nature. "Sin nature" means the image of God in us is broken, and has been replaced with a desire to be God. We still have some of the image of God, but we are dominated by sin—meaning we think and do things God would never think or do. We no longer perfectly represent who God is. The image of God is broken.

Beginning in Genesis 3 the rest of the Bible is about the restoration of the image of God in mankind. How is this done? Through Jesus Christ. Here is how it works:

1. You are to repent and believe. This is what is commonly referred to as becoming a Christian.

The time is fulfilled, and the kingdom of God is at hand; repent and believe in the gospel. - Mark 1:15

What are do you need to repent and believe? You are to repeat of disobeying God, and believe that Jesus died to pay the penalty you've earned for disobeying God. When you repent and believe God gives you a new heart and a new life. Your old, sinful self has died and been buried with Christ, and you have been born again to a new life united with Christ.

Therefore we have been buried with Him through baptism into death, so that as Christ was raised from the dead through the glory of the Father, so we too might walk in newness of life. - Romans 6:4

2. You are to become more and more like Christ, meaning that the image of God is starting to be restored in you. While on earth you cannot do this perfectly. You still fail and you still sin, but you should see steady growth toward becoming more like Christ, who is God.

For those whom He foreknew, He also predestined to become conformed to the image of His Son - Romans 8:29

What is God (Christ) like? If you are to regain the image of God, you need to know what God is like. You need to know how God thinks and behaves, and the result will be that you love like Jesus loves.

God has answered this question in scripture. For example, the

Ten Commandments are a description of the character of God. They are not just arbitrary rules. They tell you what you need to be like, if you are to have the character of God, and thus have the image of God.

Other places in scripture further describe what it means to be the image of God. In the next chapter we'll start looking at the Beatitudes, found in Jesus' most famous sermon, the Sermon on the Mount. This is what Jesus actually said and taught. From Jesus' teaching we'll learn about those attitudes and actions Jesus said will bless us and make us who we are supposed to be, the image of God.

What you'll see as we go through the Beatitudes, reading the words Jesus actually said, is that the Jesus of *Jesus Calling* is nothing like the true Jesus of scripture.

CHAPTER 18
BLESSED ARE THE POOR IN SPIRIT

The book *Jesus Calling* supposedly resulted from messages and guidance received from Jesus. It's a book that tells us what type of attitudes we should have, how we should behave, and what type of person we should be. The problem is, what *Jesus Calling* teaches does not match what scripture says. And that's a big problem.

So let's look at the real thing... the real Jesus. What does Jesus, in the Bible, say we should be like?

A good place to look is Jesus' most famous sermon, the Sermon on the Mount. It begins with a series of eight "Blessed are..." statements that describe both the road to salvation, and how to be like Christ. As Jesus proceeds through the Beatitudes, each characteristic builds on the previous ones. As a result, what we see is Jesus laying out, step-by-step, the process through which we come to salvation. This is the same process by which we grow to be more like Christ. Here is the first one:

> *Blessed are the poor in spirit, for theirs is the kingdom of heaven.*
> *- Matthew 5:3*

I've spent a lot of time doing street evangelism, which in my case means politely engaging people who are interested in having a conversation. When asked why God should let them into heaven, nearly everyone says, "Because I'm a good person." People have great self-esteem and are sure they are good enough to be acceptable to God. The problem is, this does not match reality. It is a false assurance. No one is good enough. In fact, no one is good. We are all sinners. We've all disobeyed God. (Visit: www.911Christ.com)

That is the message Jesus is giving us in the first Beatitude. None of us is good. That's why Jesus begins by telling us we need to be "poor in spirit."

Poor in spirit means to be humble. Jesus is explaining that if we desire to enter the kingdom of heaven, we cannot be full of pride about who we are or the abilities we have. We need to have a humbleness that focuses on Jesus. In particular He is telling us we must recognize there is nothing good in us. WE have NOTHING to be proud of. We are wretched sinners. When we stand before Jesus on judgment day, there is nothing we can offer Him. That's what Jesus is saying here.

For by grace you have been saved through faith; and that not of yourselves, it is the gift of God; not as a result of works, so that no one may boast.
– Ephesians 2:8 & 9

Let's imagine you are standing at the gates to heaven, applying to get in. You present your resume to God. What would be on your resume? You can't list any good deeds. When God is used as the standard of good, we have no good deeds. How about good thoughts? Nope. Again God is the standard and our thoughts are not even close to being good as defined by God. How about good recommendations? Nope, there are none. Education? Past experience? Nope. Nope. There is nothing. Your resume is blank. You have nothing you can offer that pleases God. Nothing that is acceptable to God. You cannot give God even a single reason to let you into heaven. That is what it means to be poor in spirit.

Since you have nothing you can bring to God, the only way you can enter the kingdom of heaven is when you understand that it is a free gift from God. When you repent, meaning to turn away from disobeying God, and trust in Christ Jesus as having fully paid the penalty you've earned for breaking God's law, then the free gift of salvation is yours. Then, instead of having nothing, you have Jesus. When God looks at you, instead of seeing a lawbreaker who deserves hell, He sees His Son... the perfect and righteous Jesus.

For by grace you have been saved through faith; and that not of yourselves, it is the gift of God; not as a result of works, so that no one may boast. — Ephesians 2:8 & 9

Entrance into the "kingdom of heaven"—which is another way of saying being saved—cannot be gained without being "poor in spirit."

"What is poverty of spirit? It is the opposite of that haughty, self-assertive, and self-sufficient disposition that the world so much admires and praises It is the very reverse of that independent and defiant attitude that refuses to bow to God." - A.W. Pink, The Beatitudes and the Lord's Prayer, 1979, page 15

We hear people say, "Jesus wants you to come as you are." That's true in one respect... there is nothing you can do to fix yourself, or make yourself better so that you'll be more acceptable to God. In that respect you must come to Jesus as you are, totally destitute and with nothing you can offer God.

On the other hand, there is something you must lose in order to gain entrance into the kingdom. You cannot bring your inner attitude of pride with you. You cannot bring your self-assurance that you have something you can bring to God. You cannot come as you are, full of confidence that you are good enough to enter heaven. If you think you are good enough... if you think you have something to offer God... then you are not poor in spirit. John MacArthur writes:

"As the first beatitude makes clear, entrance into the kingdom of heaven begins with being "poor in spirit," with recognition of total spiritual bankruptcy. The only way any person can come to Jesus Christ is empty-handed, totally destitute and pleading for God's mercy and grace. Without a sense of spiritual poverty, no one can enter the kingdom." - The MacArthur New Testament Commentary Matthew 1-7, 1985, page 157

We learn the same thing from other places in scripture:

The LORD is near to the brokenhearted, and saves those who are crushed in spirit. - Psalm 34:18

The sacrifices of God are a broken spirit; a broken and a contrite heart, O God, You will not despise. — Psalm 51:17

For My hand made all these things, thus all these things came into being," *declares the Lord. "But to this one I will look, to him who is humble and contrite of spirit, and who trembles at My word.* — Isaiah 66:2

You won't hear about being poor in spirit in *Jesus Calling.* Give up your pride, come to our Lord Jesus begging for His salvation.

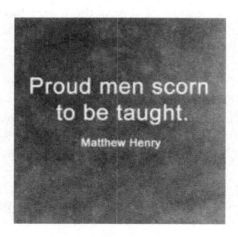

Proud men scorn to be taught.

Matthew Henry

CHAPTER 19
BLESSED ARE THOSE WHO MOURN

Is Jesus saying that in order to please Him we need to be constantly sad and crying? Are those who are empathetic, those who feel the pain of others and cry for them, are those the ones who are blessed?

In the second beatitude Jesus says:

Blessed are those who mourn, for they shall be comforted. - Matthew 5:4

To understand this verse we need to ask the question: "What is the object of the mourning we should be doing?" Why is there mourning? The answer is in scripture:

For the sorrow that is according to the will of God... produces a repentance without regret, leading to salvation, but the sorrow of the world produces death. For behold what earnestness this very thing, this godly sorrow, has produced in you: what vindication of yourselves, what indignation, what fear, what longing, what zeal, what avenging of wrong!
- 2 Corinthians 7:10-11

The sorrow, meaning the mourning, must be according to the will of God, and it must be mourning that produces repentance without regret.

What type of mourning is this?

This is mourning over sin. This is mourning over disobeying God. It is mourning over your sin and the sin of others, and it is the type of mourning that produces repentance without regret.

> *"The man who is truly Christian is a man who mourns also because of the sins of others. He does not stop at himself. He sees the same thing in others. He is concerned about the state of society, and the state of the world, and as he reads the newspaper he does not stop at what he sees or simply express disgust at it. He mourns because of it... He knows that it is all due to sin; and he mourns because of it."* – D. Martin Lloyd-Jones, Studies In The Sermon On The Mount, page 48

One of the most often memorized verses in the Bible is John 11:35, *"Jesus wept."* This verse is part of the story of Lazarus, who lay dead and decaying in a tomb for four days before Jesus raised him from the dead.

Why did Jesus weep?

Yes, he was weeping out of love for Lazarus. But, He knew Lazarus would soon be alive again. Jesus was primarily weeping because He was filled with grief over the deadly effects of the sin He saw in the people around Him. Jesus was mourning over sin. Do you mourn and weep over your sin?

Being poor in spirit means we understand we are sinners and that we have nothing good in us, nor is there anything we can do to please God. This leads us to Godly sorrow over sin. We mourn over our sin, as well as the sin that is saturating the world. And our Godly mourning leads to repentance... a turning away from sin and toward obeying God. Mourning over sin leads to our rejecting sin and seeking to obey God in everything.

This IS truly Jesus calling us to mourn over sin.

CHAPTER 20
BLESSED ARE THE MEEK

Blessed are the meek, for they shall inherit the earth.
- Matthew 5:5 (KJV)

We think of meek and gentle people as being the losers. Those who do not stand up for themselves. Those who get pushed around by stronger people. Our big-screen heroes are those who are bold, those who refuse to submit to authority, and those who believe they are right and who act on that belief and are victorious... and at the end of the film they get the love of a beautiful woman. The winners! Those who are meek get nothing.

But the humble [meek] *will inherit the land, and will delight themselves in abundant prosperity.* - Psalm 37:11

The meek will inherit the earth? That does not make sense... until we recognize that Jesus is talking about spiritual attributes. Jesus was strong and bold. He did not cower before the leading Jews of His day, the scribes and Pharisees. He called them hypocrites, vipers, and white-washed tombs—good looking on the outside, but with death inside. He drove the sellers of sacrificial animals and money changers from the Temple, overturning their tables in the process. (John 2:14-15; Matthew 21:12-13)

Jesus was not weak, but He was meek. The meekness Jesus is talking about in this third beatitude is strength under control.

109

Here's a question: From what we have seen so far in the beatitudes, is Jesus talking about the physical or the spiritual? Is he talking about the way we are on the outside, or on the inside?

Jesus is focusing on the internal. Our thoughts, our attitudes... our spiritual life. So, what does it mean to have an internal attitude of meekness... an attitude of Godly meekness?

Looking at the original Greek word is helpful here. The Greek word translated as "meek" or sometimes as "gentle," is also used to describe a wild animal that has been "broken" so the animal can be useful to man. The example we're most familiar with is that of a wild horse being broken so it can ridden.

When a horse is broken, what has changed? Has its physical strength changed? No. What has changed is the horse's attitude... from an attitude of wildness and self-centeredness... to an attitude of gentleness. The power and strength is still there, but it is completely under control.

> *"True meekness is not weakness. A striking proof of this is furnished in Acts 16:35-37. The apostles had been wrongly beaten and cast into prison. On the next day the magistrates gave orders for their release, but Paul said to their agents, 'Let them come themselves and fetch us out.' God-given meekness can stand up for God-given rights."* - A.W. Pink, The Beatitudes and The Lord's Prayer, 1979, page 28.

When Jesus says *"blessed are the meek"* He is saying that those who have submitted to God... those who no longer seek to do what they desire, but instead seek to do what God desires... those are the people who will be blessed and will inherit the earth.

> *Therefore I, the prisoner of the Lord, implore you to walk in a manner worthy of the calling with which you have been called, with all humility and gentleness, with patience, showing tolerance for one another in love, being diligent to preserve the unity of the Spirit in the bond of peace.* - Ephesians 4:1-3

Jesus was not weak. Meekness does not mean to be without power... it means strength under control. Strength that serves God, not our selfish desires.

Like a city that is broken into and without walls, is a man who has no control over his spirit. - Proverbs 25:28

He who is slow to anger is better than the mighty, and he who rules his spirit, than he who captures a city. - Proverbs 16:32

Those who are meek are in control of their emotions and their strength, and they use their resources according to the will of God as revealed in scripture.

This IS the true Jesus calling you to submit your will to God.

CHAPTER 21
BLESSED ARE THOSE WHO
HUNGER & THIRST FOR RIGHTEOUSNESS

I recently went on a diet. I began exercising, and I cut back from five meals per day, with various snacks in between, to just three regular-sized meals per day. The result was that I'd eat a meal, and still be hungry. I went to bed hungry. I woke up hungry. I was hungry all the time. No problem, I thought. I have will-power.

But, by the third week I was ready to give it up. Will-power or no, I was hungry. My wife was gone for the day. No one was around. And I ate the dish of cookies she had left on the kitchen counter. It was her fault, she left them out! (Didn't Adam say something like that, when he was held accountable by God?)

We are to hunger for righteousness... hunger for sin to be gone... in the same way we hunger for food when we're starving. Going on a diet for a couple of weeks is not close to having the level of hunger and thirst Jesus is talking about.

Image it's a hot day. Early that morning you started out on a short hike. But, now you are lost, and you've not had anything to drink all day. Your tongue feels like sandpaper. Your lips are cracked. You've got a headache. All you can think about is a cool bottle of Crystal Springs water. But, night comes, there is no rescue, and no water.

The next day is even hotter. Your every thought is about water. If only there was a drop of water for your tongue. Just a single drop. That would be some relief. But, there is none. You are thirsty... you desire water more than anything else. All you can think about is getting just one small drink. It is your ONLY desire. You can't go on unless you get some water!!! Just a little!! Just a few drops!!! PLEASE!!! Now we are getting to the level of thirsting Jesus is talking about when He says:

Blessed are those who hunger and thirst for righteousness, for they will be filled. - Matthew 5:6

Jesus is talking about a desire for righteousness that has the intensity of a starving man's desire for food.

Our normal desires are focused on ourselves. We hunger and thirst for the physical necessities of life, as well as things that are not necessary. Our human desires are to satisfy ourselves, whether it is for necessities such as food and shelter, or things such as respect and fame. Sometimes we desire for others to desire what we have—we desire that they be jealous of us. But those who hunger and thirst for righteousness, they desire, above all else, to obey and glorify God. Their focus is on God and on righteousness, not on themselves.

"We have realized that in this Beatitude we begin to turn away from an examination of self, to God. This is, of course, a vital matter, for it is this whole question of how to turn to God that causes many to stumble... Unless we 'hunger and thirst' after righteousness, we shall never have it, we shall never know the fullness which is here promised to us... the very essence of the Christian salvation is given us in this verse. It is a perfect statement of the doctrine of salvation by grace only." - D. Martin Lloyd- Jones, Studies In the Sermon on The Mount, 1976, page 71

But thanks be to God that, though you used to be slaves to sin, you have come to obey from your heart the pattern of teaching that has now claimed your allegiance. You have been set free from sin and have become slaves to righteousness. — Romans 6:17-18

They have become slaves to righteousness? What does that mean? What is righteousness? The dictionary definition of righteousness is: *"behavior that is morally justifiable or right."* But, if we look at a Bible dictionary we get a somewhat different definition:

"God is righteousness....All of God's acts are righteous.... Because God

is righteous, he expects righteousness of others, who are to reflect the nature of their creator. The expected response to God's rule is....conformity to His rule and will." - Tyndale Bible Dictionary, 2001, page 1134

The character of God defines righteousness. We are created in His image and need to conform to His character. But, that's impossible!

Yes, it is impossible for us, but not for God. Through the cross God has assigned Christ's righteousness to us. We are not righteous, but as Christians we have the righteousness of Christ. And as Christians our hunger and thirst is for righteousness. And that driving desire for righteousness makes us willing slaves of righteousness... continually striving to put off sin, and put on the new life we have in Christ.

"As slaves of righteousness, our entire being has been rescued and reoriented under the authority of Christ. Through the work of the Spirit, we are being conformed into Christ's character and refined for the work of His kingdom." - Jeremiah Johnson, Slaves To Righteousness, http://tiny.cc/6kh34x

What is righteousness? It is simply conformity to Christ's character. Jesus Christ is righteousness. Blessed are those who hunger and thirst to be like Jesus in every way.

He made Him who knew no sin to be sin on our behalf, so that we might become the righteousness of God in Him. – 2 Corinthians 5:21

Just as food and water is required for us to stay physically alive, righteousness is required for us to be spiritually alive. Just as food and water are not optional, righteousness is not optional for spiritual life.

"Hunger and thirst represent the necessities of physical life. Jesus' analogy demonstrates that righteousness is required for spiritual life just as food and water are required for physical life. Righteousness is not an optional spiritual supplement but a spiritual necessity. We can no more live spiritually without righteousness than we can live physically without food and water." - John MacArthur, The MacArthur New Testament Commentary Matthew 1-7, 1985, page 178

But seek first His kingdom and His righteousness... - Matthew 6:33

God's character describes righteousness. God's law, such as the Ten Commandments describe God's character. Scripture gives us God's law, describing the righteousness we should hunger and thirst after. We need to be in God's word, reading and studying scripture and then applying it to our lives. That is the result of hungering and thirsting for righteousness.

Why do you spend money for what is not bread, and your wages for what does not satisfy? Listen carefully to Me, and eat what is good, And delight yourself in abundance. Incline your ear and come to Me. - Isaiah 55:2-3a

The true Jesus is calling you to righteousness.

CHAPTER 22
BLESSED ARE THE MERCIFUL

Blessed are the merciful, for they will be shown mercy. – Matthew 5:7

Mercy is a characteristic of both God and of those who are in God's kingdom. Without God's mercy, it would be over, we'd all be headed to hell.

> *"In the first four beatitudes a definite progression of spiritual awakening and transformation has been noted as one of the thrusts of our Lord's teaching. First there is a discovery of the fact that I am nothing—poverty of spirit. Second, there is conviction of sin, a consciousness of guilt producing godly sorrow—mourning. Third, there is a renouncing of self-dependence and a taking of my place in the dust before God—meekness. Fourth, there follows an intense longing after Christ and His salvation—hunger and thirsting for righteousness... In the next four Beatitudes we come to the manifestation of positive good in the believer, the fruits of a new creation and the blessings of a transformed character."* - A.W. Pink, The Beatitudes and the Lord's Prayer, 1979, page 37.

There is a pattern to the beatitudes. The first four beatitudes are about internal attitudes, about ourselves and about God. The first four show that what we are inside is what counts—right thinking. Later in the Sermon on the Mount Jesus will give examples showing that it is our internal attitude that matters, such as anger being the same as murder, and lust being adultery.

116

1. Right Prayer

2. Right Thinking

3. Right Action

These next four beatitudes are about the external... about our actions. Each of the first four Beatitudes are directly related to the last four. This is an important principle: We cannot have right actions unless we have right attitudes. The first four Beatitudes tell us what the right attitudes are. In the next four beatitudes we'll see the actions that result from those right attitudes.

John MacArthur explains how mercy is related to being poor in spirit:

"Those who are in poverty of spirit recognize their need for mercy and are led to show mercy to others." - The MacArthur New Testament Commentary Matthew 1-7, 1985, page 187

But that's not what comes naturally...

Since the fall people have essentially been focused on themselves. Self-concern characterizes humanity. We see this in such sayings as: *"If you don't look out for yourself, no one else will."*

What is mercy?

Mercy results from love, and is compassion in action. It is our taking action to give help to the helpless who are in need.

Jesus Christ is the perfect example of mercy. He is the most merciful human who ever lived—perfect mercy. He reached out to heal the sick, restore the crippled, give sight to the blind, hearing to the deaf, and even life to the dead. Jesus wept with those in sorrow and gave companionship to the lonely.

What is mercy? Mercy is the result of love. Jesus is love, and because of His love, He has mercy on us.

But God, being rich in mercy, because of His great love with which He loved us, even when we were dead in our transgressions, made us alive together with Christ (by grace you have been saved), – Ephesians 2:4-5

If we are to understand mercy, we must understand love. Biblical love is not a feeling, it is an action. Mercy is one of the actions produced by love. Here are some of the characteristics of mercy:

- Mercy is not feeling compassion. Mercy is doing something about another person's poor condition.

- Mercy is not voting for government welfare programs. Mercy is your taking action to help other people with their needs.

- Mercy is not giving people whatever they want. Mercy is helping the helpless with their true needs.

- Mercy is not just forgiving someone who has harmed you, and then putting them out of your mind and "moving on." Mercy means reaching out to your enemies and helping to meet their true needs.

An important principle is that mercy is not giving someone whatever they ask for, but giving them what they need. For example, no matter how much they plead for one, it is not merciful to buy an alcoholic a drink. That may be what they want, but it's not what they need.

How would you show mercy to an alcoholic? First, recognize they may not want your mercy. In that case, it may be that all you can do is pray for them. (And by the way, prayer is powerful. When you pray you are doing a lot for them.)

If an alcoholic wants help, mercy would be to direct them to a Biblical addiction recovery counselor or group. Then drive them to their appointment, and even go to the meeting with them. Pray with them after the appointment, and be someone they can call whenever they feel the urge to take a drink. That is the loving thing to do... sacrificial giving to meet true needs. That is true mercy.

What about when someone has harmed you? How do you respond with mercy?

Mercy begins with forgiveness, but it doesn't stop there. For example, God's mercy did not stop with forgiving your sin, His mercy dealt with the entire problem. Forgiving a criminal does not save them from the punishment for their crime. There still must be justice. It's the same with God. The mercy God gave you not only included forgiveness, but also included justice. Jesus took on Himself the punishment you deserved, paying the penalty you earned when He died on the cross.

Justice means the penalty for breaking the law must be paid.

For example, imagine I've committed a major crime and I'm standing before a judge. Let's even say the crime was breaking into the judge's home, trashing it, stealing everything of value, smashing his cars, and stealing his identity and selling it to a Chinese crime syndicate. At the end of the trial the judge looks at me and says, "You are guilty, but I forgive you."

Does that mean I go free? No, I still must pay the penalty for what I've done wrong. That is justice.

And that's what Jesus did on the cross. He died on the cross, taking on Himself the full wrath of God for your sin. You deserved God's wrath. That is justice for your breaking God's laws. God could not just say, "I forgive you." and let you go free. So what He did was to take on Himself the punishment you deserved. He paid your fine, so to speak. That is true mercy!

"If we have received from a holy God unlimited mercy that cancels our unpayable debt of sin—we who had no righteousness but were poor in spirit, mourning over our load of sin in beggarly, helpless condition, wretched and doomed, meek before almighty God, hungry and thirsty for righteousness we did not have and could not attain—it surely follows that we should be merciful to others." - The MacArthur New Testament Commentary Matthew 1-7, 1985, page 197

Be merciful, just as your Father is merciful. - Luke 6:36

For judgment will be merciless to one who has shown no mercy; - James 2:13

Blessed be the God and Father of our Lord Jesus Christ, who according to His great mercy has caused us to be born again to a living hope through the resurrection of Jesus Christ from the dead, - 1 Peter 1:3

What is everyone's greatest need? The gospel—God's mercy. If someone is not trusting in Jesus Christ as their savior, their greatest need is the Gospel. If you tell them about Jesus and the Gospel, it is the greatest act of love and mercy that anyone can do for another.

This IS truly Jesus calling, offering you His forgiveness and mercy.

CHAPTER 23
BLESSED ARE THE PURE IN HEART

Blessed are the pure in heart, for they will see God. - Matthew 5:8

What did God just say? These are amazing words. They should leave you in awe... you will see God. What an incredible promise!

Jesus Calling talks about being in the presence of God, mentioning that it is like being enveloped in a warm mist. The real Jesus promises the truth... you will see God... live... face-to-face... in person... God, who can hold the entire universe in the palm of His hand (Isaiah 40:12) and who knows the names of all the stars (Isaiah 40:26). God, who created everything by just speaking it into existence. God, who knows your every thought. God, who is perfect and pure, and holy. Yes, that God. You will see that God.

When I picture myself in heaven I see myself as a file clerk in a basement room. There is just one small window, up high on the wall behind my desk. If I stand on my tippy toes I can just see out the window... and far away I can see God's glory glowing on the other side of a far-away hill. I'm too much of a sinner to be any closer to God. But, God says that's a lie! You will see God! It is both frightening and incredibly awesome. You will see God!!!

"The great reception is at hand; in a sense the ceremony is all prepared; you and I are waiting for the audience with the King. Are you looking forward to it? Are you preparing yourself for it? Don't you feel ashamed at this

moment that you are wasting your time on things that not only will be of no value to you on that great occasion, but of which you will then be ashamed. You and I, creatures of time as we appear to be, are going to see God and bask in His eternal glory for ever and ever. Our one confidence is that He is working in us and preparing us for that. But let us also work and purify ourselves 'even as he is pure.'" - D. Martin Lloyd-Jones, Studies In The Sermon On The Mount, 1976, page 99

Imagine it. You will see God, if you are pure in heart. All believers will see God.

And everyone who has this hope fixed on Him [Jesus] *purifies himself, just as He is pure.* - 1 John 3:3

In the Bible the "heart" is the center of who you are. It includes your mind, your desires, your personality, and your character. It is who you are and what you think.

For as he thinks within himself, so he is. - Proverbs 23:7

"Why are you thinking evil in your hearts?" - Jesus speaking in Matthew 9:4

To be "pure in heart" means to have pure thoughts, pure desires, pure feelings, and a pure character.

Watch over your heart with all diligence, for from it flow the springs of life. - Proverbs 4:23

What does it mean to have a "pure" heart?

When a metal is made pure, it is refined to remove all impurities. A pure metal is one composed of just one type of metal. There is no contamination. This is what Jesus is talking about, but applied to your heart instead of metal. He is telling us to be single-minded. We need to have a single-minded devotion to God, and a single-minded devotion to obeying God. If we have desires to serve both the Lord, and follow the world, that is double-mindedness. That's not being pure in heart, and it won't work. Later in the Sermon on the Mount

Jesus says:

> *No one can serve two masters; for either he will hate the one and love the other, or he will be devoted to one and despise the other. You cannot serve God and wealth.* - Matthew 6:24

James puts the same truth another way...

> *You adulteresses, do you not know that friendship with the world is hostility toward God? Therefore whoever wishes to be a friend of the world makes himself an enemy of God.* - James 4:4

Then in verse 8 James gives the solution to the problem.... how we can become pure in our hearts:

> *Draw near to God and He will draw near to you. Cleanse your hands, you sinners; and purify your hearts, you double-minded.* - James 4:8

How do we draw near to God? Cleanse yourself. Have a pure heart—a single minded devotion to God and obeying God. Is this in any way similar to coming into the presence of Jesus as described in *Jesus Calling*? No.

As we become pure in heart, the result is that we will draw near to God. Why? Because we have turned away from sin. Sin is always the problem, and it is sin that separates us from God. Only when we become pure in heart can we draw near to God.

> *A holy person's motivating aim, passion, desire, longing, aspiration, goal, and drive is to please God, both by what one does and by what one avoids doing. In other words, one practices good works and cuts out evil ones.* – J.I. Packer, Rediscovering Holiness, 1992, page 22

The Biblical idea of drawing near to God is not in any way similar to what *Jesus Calling* refers to as coming into the presence of Jesus. If you've read *Jesus Calling* you may have noticed there is little about sin. Yet, sin is the problem. If we don't deal with sin, we can never come into the presence of our Lord Jesus Christ.

How do we deal with sin? We can't. Sin means we've broken God's laws and must pay the just penalty, eternity in hell. Only Jesus

Christ can save us. By dying on the cross he paid the penalty we owe for sin, and He freely offers His work on the cross to us. If you repent (turn away from law-breaking) and accept the gift God offers, it is yours. Then you can draw near to God.

Are we perfectly pure of heart after we are saved? No. We still sin. We still desire some of what the world offers. So we are still double-minded... not pure. What can we do? Continue to live out the beatitudes. And when you sin, repent and confess your sin to God.

What does drawing near to God mean?

Since the presence of God is such a big part of *Jesus* Calling, let's see what scripture says about drawing near to God:

- First, it means we are saved. Being pure in heart and our salvation are both gifts from God, and they go together. We cannot become pure in heart through our own efforts. And we cannot be saved through own efforts. It is through trusting that Jesus paid our penalty for sin that we receive these gifts and can then draw near to God. It is the foundation of our relationship with God. (Hebrews 10:19-22)

- Drawing near to God means loving Him with all your heart, and with all your soul, and with all your mind (Matthew 22:37). As we learned in Chapter 17, that means obeying God.

- Drawing near to God means walking in the will of the Holy Spirit (Galatians 5:16). This means to not only desire to obey God, but striving to obey God in all your thoughts and actions.

- Drawing near to God means knowing God, and that means being in God's word. No one can draw near to God without being deeply in God's word. If you are not spending time in God's word, you will not know God nor His will.

What does being in God's word mean? Reading four pages every day? Reading a chapter a day? Reading through the Bible in a year? Yes, it could be any of these, or all of them, or something different.

o   What it means is reading and understanding God's word, whatever the reading plan you use. There are various approaches that can be used, such as:

o   Reading one book in the Old Testament, and then one book in the New Testament.

o   Memorizing scripture is excellent and should be a part of any Bible reading plan.

o   Reading a chapter a day is another good approach. You'll be surprised at how quickly you'll get through the entire Bible.

o   Reading one book, or several chapters from a larger book, once a day, every day for a week. Reading the same scripture several days in a row will help you go deeper into God's word.

o   Do not skip around, reading random verses each day. Have a reading plan that allows you to get an understanding of each book, as well as the overall flow through the entire Bible.

Whatever approach you use, get help with understanding scripture. Being a part of a Bible study group can be helpful. Or use your church library as a source of commentaries and reference books. Plus spend time meditating about what you've read. Fill your head with scripture and then consider how what you've just read fits with the rest of scripture, and how it applies to your life.

Do not be conformed to this world, but be transformed by the renewal of your mind, that by testing you may discern what is the will of God, what is good and acceptable and perfect. — Romans 12:2

•   Finally, drawing near to God means being in prayer. Not frivolous prayer, but a serious conversation of thanks,

worship, and petition.
With all prayer and petition pray at all times in the Spirit.
- Ephesians 6:18

What do we pray? We could pray with David:

Create in me a clean heart, O God, - Psalm 51:10

Who may ascend into the hill of the Lord? And who may stand in His holy place? He who has clean hands and a pure heart, - Psalm 24:3-4

But, there is one other fact we need to deal with. We are fallen. We are broken. That means that in this life we can never achieve perfect purity. We need the purity of Christ.

Who can say, "I have cleansed my heart, I am pure from my sin"?
- Proverbs 20:9

The assumed answer to the above question in scripture is, "No one." Because we are fallen we cannot become pure through our own efforts. The answer is to trust in Christ's purity. Trust in Christ's righteousness. When you are saved He gives His purity and His righteousness to you.

Jesus is calling you to have a pure heart—a purity that only comes with salvation. Jesus is calling you to trust in Him as our savior from the wrath of God. And as a result you will receive the righteousness of Christ and the pure heart only Christ can give you.

This is Jesus calling you to turn to Him. Trust that He has paid your penalty for sin. And He will give you a pure heart.

CHAPTER 24
BLESSED ARE THE PEACEMAKERS

Jesus offers true peace and expects we'll share that peace with others. All Christians are called to be peacemakers. That means sharing the peace of Christ with others by telling them about Jesus Christ and the gospel. It also means being a peacemaker in your family, neighborhood, and to as wide a circle of people as you can reach.

This connotes both peace with God and peace between people—the latter flows out of the former. Jesus is the supreme peacemaker, who reconciles human beings with God through the cross (Colossians 1:20), so the supreme peacemaking is the proclamation of the gospel. - Grant Osborne, Exegetical Commentary on Matthew, 2010, page 168.

Men are without peace because they are without God, the source of peace." - John MacArthur, The MacArthur New Testament Commentary, Matthew 1-7, 1985, page 213

"The great enemy of peace is sin. Sin separates men from God and causes disharmony and enmity with Him. And man's lack of harmony with God causes their lack of harmony with each other.... To talk of peace without talking of repentance of sin is to talk foolishly and vainly." - John MacArthur, The MacArthur New Testament Commentary, Matthew 1-7, 1985, page 212

Blessed are the peacemakers, for they will be called children of God. - Matthew 5:9

Understanding what Jesus means by "peace" is crucial. The Greek word translated as "peace" in the Beatitudes (Matthew 5:9) is used in only one other place in the Bible, in Colossians 1:20 where Paul talks about the cross:

"...and through Him to reconcile all things to Himself, having made peace through the blood of His cross;" - Colossians 1:20

As Christians we are to be peacemakers, working to bring harmony to the world. But, peace is only temporary without the cross. For true peace there must first be peace between men and God. A peace that only comes through the cross.

What type of peace is this?

We are all born as enemies of God. Born as children of Satan. That means we are children of God's wrath:

You adulteresses, do you not know that friendship with the world is hostility toward God? Therefore whoever wishes to be a friend of the world makes himself an enemy of God. - James 4:4

For if while we were enemies we were reconciled to God through the death of His Son, - Romans 5:10

You are of your father the devil, and you want to do the desires of your father. - John 8:44

The natural man is a child of wrath... an enemy of God. You may feel very spiritual, and you may even be very religious, but you are still an enemy of God... someone without the peace of God.

What is peace with God?

In *Jesus Calling* peace is a feeling. It is a feeling of relaxation, safety, and calmness. That is not the peace of the Bible. In scripture peace

128

is a condition. It is the condition of no longer being at war with God, and instead being in harmony with God. It is a condition of no longer being in conflict with God, but being in agreement with God. As a result of being at peace with God, you will have the fruit of the Spirit, which includes a feeling of peace and contentment.

Bringing peace to the world.

Who are the peace markers Jesus is saying are blessed? At the head of the list are those who help the children of wrath make peace with God. Christians are commissioned (Matthew 28:16-20) to bring peace to the children of wrath, by bringing them the gospel... the good news about salvation through the cross of Christ.

. What is the message we bring? Because of what Christ did on the cross you can have peace by repenting and trusting Jesus Christ as your savior. Peacemakers are those who tell others about Jesus and the gospel.

But, don't be surprised if you do not get the results you expect. Our efforts to bring peace between men and God often result in conflict and a less peaceful world.

"Do not think that I came to bring peace on the earth; I did not come to bring peace, but a sword." - Matthew 10:34

Why would Jesus say this? Why is it that for there to be true and lasting peace there first must be more conflict?

Because the world hates the Gospel. The world rebels against the Gospel. Although it is only through the Gospel that there can be the righteousness that brings peace, the world wants nothing to do with the gospel

As Christians we need to be working to bring peace among people, this is called being the salt of the earth. But, true lasting peace only comes through the cross, through people being born again with a new heart and new life. A new life based on these eight beatitudes, not on a book like *Jesus Calling.*

"There is no peace like the peace of those whose minds are possessed with full assurance that they have known God, and God has known them, and that this relationship guarantees God's favour to them in life, through death, and

on forever." – J.I. Packer, Knowing God, 1973, page 26

Christians are also peacemakers among men. Although there can be no lasting peace among men without the gospel, we are still to work to reduce conflict and fighting among individuals, as well as nations.

However, the focus is always on the gospel, even as we help our neighbors to get along with each other. This is crucially important: there is no permanent peace without the gospel. For there to be peace, we must tell people about the Gospel.

Therefore, having been justified by faith, we have peace with God through our Lord Jesus Christ – Romans 5:1

Blessed are the peacemakers. Reject the false peace of *Jesus Calling*. Go out and be a true peacemaker today. Tell someone about how Jesus has delivered you from the penalty for sin.

CHAPTER 25
BLESSED ARE THOSE WHO ARE
PERSECUTED BECAUSE OF RIGHTEOUSNESS

Here's some "good" news... if you are a true Christian, you will be persecuted. You will have troubles. People will hate you. Isn't that great?

Indeed, all who desire to live godly in Christ Jesus will be persecuted.
- 2 Timothy 3:12

Blessed are those who are persecuted because of righteousness, for theirs is the kingdom of heaven. - Matthew 5:10

This verse is commonly interpreted to mean: if you stand up for what is right, that's a good thing and you will go to heaven. But, that's a worldly view of this Beatitude, and not at all what Jesus is saying.

Or those who are in a Christian cult say, *"You've just called my religion a cult. I'm being persecuted. That means my religion is the right one. That I'm being 'persecuted' for my faith proves it!"* This also is not what Jesus is saying.

If we continue reading in Matthew, Jesus makes it clear what He is talking about:

Blessed are you when people insult you, persecute you and falsely say all kinds of evil against you because of me. Rejoice and be glad, because great is your reward in heaven, for in the same way they persecuted the prophets who were before you. – Matthew 5:11-12

131

Jesus first states that those who are persecuted because of righteousness will be blessed. He follows that with a clear definition of righteousness—He is righteousness. Jesus is righteousness. But, only the true Jesus is righteous. The "Jesus" of *Jesus Calling* is not the true Jesus and thus is not an example of righteousness.

> **What is your reward** for being poor in spirit, mourning over sin, being meek, and hungering and thirsting for righteousness? What is your reward for being merciful, pure of heart, and a peacemaker? What is your reward for all this? **You will be persecuted.**

Why are true Christians persecuted?

When Jesus Christ was on earth the world hated him. He was despised, constantly challenged, and finally beaten, scourged, and crucified. If Christ was persecuted, why should we think we'll receive anything less?

For to you it has been granted on behalf of Christ, not only to believe in Him, but also to suffer for His sake. - Philippians 1:29

That I may know Him and the power of His resurrection, and the fellowship of His sufferings, being conformed to His death. - Philippians 3:10

You will be persecuted because you are obeying God. Persecution means you are living the kingdom life... you are living the way people in the kingdom should live... and that means you will be blessed. BUT... the world does not like people who are obeying God.

When you act like Christ... when you live out the righteousness of Christ, you will share in the persecution of Christ.

To live for Christ is to live in opposition to Satan, and to his world... and to his world system. And that means those in the world system will hate you. They will preach love, but hate Jesus. They will talk about peace, but will seek to silence Jesus, even if it means crucifying Him. But since they can't get at Jesus their hatred turns to those who follow Jesus... you.

To be like Christ—and that is our goal—will bring the same result it has throughout history... and the same result it brought to Christ when He lived on earth. Persecution.

The Beatitudes, and the Sermon on the Mount, are about righteousness, and by its very nature righteousness confronts wickedness. And that brings persecution. The Puritan writer Thomas Watson wrote the following about Christians:

> *"Though they be ever so meek, merciful, pure in heart, their piety will not shield them from sufferings. They must hang their harp on the willows and take the cross. The way to heaven is by way of thorns and blood. Though it be full of roses in regard of the comforts of the Holy Ghost, yet it is full of thorns in regard of persecutions."* — Thomas Watson, Discourses On Important and Interesting Subjects, Volume 2, 1829, page 348

Persecution is not incidental to a faithful Christian lifestyle, it is certain. In 1 Thessalonians chapter 2 Paul mentions persecution and how he has been hindered by persecution. In chapter 3 he says this is to be expected...

> *"...so that no one would be disturbed by these afflictions; for you yourselves know that we have been destined for this. For indeed when we were with you, we kept telling you in advance that we were going to suffer affliction; and so it came to pass, as you know.* — 1 Thessalonians 3:3-4

There is a simple way to avoid persecution... live like the world. Do whatever the world does... fit in with everyone around you. Or if that's more than you can do, then just keep your mouth shut and have an attitude of "live and let live." Don't make waves.

Living like the world may even seem like it costs nothing, and it has the benefit of avoiding trials, troubles, confrontation, and conflict. That's all good, right? It makes life easier, right? But, what are you doing? You are turning your back on Christ, you are turning your back on God and losing your spiritual purity and righteousness. That's a huge cost.

For churches and church leaders there may seem to be no other option. The worldly benefits in keeping quiet far outweigh the benefits of preaching the gospel. Preaching the gospel may insult some people in the church. You may lose a part of your congregation, and the associated income. Preaching the gospel may strain the church's relationship with the community. You don't want to do that. So just keep quiet about the reality of sin. Don't tell people that apart from the saving power of the gospel they remain in their sins and are destined for hell. And what do you get? A church that has turned its back on the mission God has called the church to do. A church that has rejected God in order to please man.

If we live as Christians should, having the righteousness of Christ, then we are truly following Jesus as we cry out to the world that Jesus Christ is the way... the only way to salvation. And scripture says this will bring persecution that results in your being blessed.

> *Blessed are those who are persecuted because of righteousness, for theirs is the kingdom of heaven.* - Matthew 5:10

> By grace God makes men vessels of silver and vessels of gold, and then casts them into the fire to melt and suffer for His name, and a higher glory He cannot put upon them on this side of glory.
>
> **Thomas Brooks**

CHAPTER 26
RUN FROM FALSE TEACHERS

Beloved, do not believe every spirit, but test the spirits to see whether they are from God. - 1 John 4:1

What I have tried to do in this book is to be obedient to scripture and test the spirits... test *Jesus Calling* to see if it is truly of God. It did not pass the test.

After reading this book, how do you feel you should treat *Jesus Calling*? Should you continue reading it? Should you recommend or give copies to friends? Should you give it to your young nieces and nephews?

Or should you stop reading it, but keep the copy you have... just in case you'd like to look at it again when you need an emotional boost? Or maybe you should donate your copy to Goodwill?

Or should you throw away your copy of *Jesus Calling*, and recommend that your friends do the same.

What should you do?

To answer that question we need to determine how scripture classifies *Jesus Calling*. Is it harmless, and of no concern? Is it Biblical enough to be used? Is it heretical and dangerous? Is it non-Christian and can be ignored?

Jesus Calling presents itself as a Christian book, and it presents "Jesus" teaching us how we should think and live. This is serious. If it is anything other than the Christian book it claims to be, it is false teaching and should be treated as such.

I hope I have clearly shown that *Jesus Calling* is false teaching.

How are we to respond to false teaching?

Run from it! Do not bring it into your house. Do not read it. Do not allow even a tiny bit of its teaching into your heart. Here is what scripture says:

> *Beware of the false prophets, who come to you in sheep's clothing, but inwardly are ravenous wolves.* – Matthew 7:15

> *Anyone who does not remain in Christ's teaching but goes beyond it, does not have God. The one who remains in that teaching, this one has both the Father and the Son. If anyone comes to you and does not bring this teaching, do not receive him into your house, and do not give him a greeting; for the one who gives him a greeting participates in his evil deeds.* - 2 John 10-11

Did you get that? Do not even allow false teachers into your home. Dom not extend hospitality to false teachers. Why does John say this? Because, not only will false teaching hinder you from knowing and obeying the truth. Showing hospitality to false teachers, or having a book like *Jesus Calling* in your home, will indicate to others that you approve of the false teaching. You will be telling other that *Jesus Calling* is an okay book for them to read.

Working in the area of apologetics I have quite a few books about cults, false religions, and other types of heresy and false teaching. I keep them together in a single section of my bookcase. Prominently placed on one of the shelves are several pairs of industrial safety glasses. When a visitor looks at these books, I tell them they must wear the proper personal protection equipment, and I hand them a pair of safety glasses. That makes the point that these are not good books.

> *You were running well; who hindered you from obeying the truth? This persuasion did not come from Him who calls you. A little leaven leavens the whole lump of dough.* — Galatians 5:7b-9

This is what scriptures says about false teaching: Don't listen to false teaching. Don't read it, and don't share it with anyone. Don't even bring it into your home. Don't expose yourself to it. And don't do or say anything that might indicate you approve it, or any part of it, as that might encourage other Christians to be deceived by the false teaching.

Yes, there is some truth.

False teaching always contains some truth. Sometimes even a majority of the teaching is true. But, that does not make it good nor acceptable. Even a small amount of falsehood poisons the entire book. As Galatians says, *"A little leaven leavens the whole lump of dough."*

Does this mean we turn away from and reject anyone who has an error in their teaching? No. None of us are perfect, and no human teaching, no matter how good or Biblical, will be completely free from error.

But, if a book is presenting a different Jesus, or a different gospel, it is false teaching and should be totally rejected. If a book is leading people away from the true Jesus or the true gospel, it is false teaching. If a teaching does not glorify God, it is a false teaching.

That is what we have in the devotional book *Jesus Calling*. This is a different Jesus and a different gospel. This book leads people away from Jesus, not toward Him. It is not a book that glorifies God, it blasphemes God. This is a book to run from. Get it out of your home. Don't give away your copy, as it may harm someone else. The only answer is the trash bin.

BUT… *Jesus Calling* really helped me. BUT… *Jesus calling* includes scripture. BUT… *Jesus Calling* does have some Biblically correct information. BUT… *it was a gift from my great grandmother.* None of these are reasons for keeping your copy of *Jesus Calling*. It may sound "Christian," but it presents a false Jesus. The "Jesus" of *Jesus Calling* is a feminized, new-age, mystical Jesus who is more concerned about being your friend than he is about sin, righteousness, the gospel, and truly loving you.

> *In today's world there are many false "Christs" seeking our devotion. But there will come that moment when the true Christ will appear, and those who are following a false 'Christ' will find out they have been deceived. Yet perhaps the most amazing thing about all this is that we have the opportunity right now—while there is still time—to pray and ask God to correct us if we are in any way being deceived. And we need to test the spirits just as the Bible instructs us to do.* - Warren B. Smith, Another Jesus Calling, 2013, page 130

There is only one option when it comes to *Jesus Calling*, RUN! Get rid of your copy of *Jesus Calling*. Throw it in the trash. And tell others this is a book they should avoid. This book is particularly dangerous for non-believers, and those who may think they are Christians, but are not. They are easily deceived. Instead of a savior, the picture of Jesus they'll get from *Jesus Calling* is that of a god who cares more about their comfort today than he does about their eternal soul.

It's NOT JESUS CALLING!!!!

CHAPTER 27
WHAT'S THE BIG DEAL ABOUT THE CROSS?

Jesus is God. Why would God make Himself human, come to earth... and then allow Himself to be killed in a very painful and undignified manner when He was only 33 years old? Does this make sense? What good is a dead Messiah? He couldn't even save Himself.

There is a very good reason why Jesus did what He did. Scripture explains that Jesus' purpose was to come to save the lost:

For the Son of Man has come to seek and to save that which was lost.
- Luke 19:10

It is a trustworthy statement, deserving full acceptance, that Christ Jesus came into the world to save sinners – 1 Timothy 1:15

For even the Son of Man did not come to be served, but to serve, and to give His life a ransom for many. – Mark 10:45

Jesus answered, "You say correctly that I am a king. For this I have been born, and for this I have come into the world, to testify to the truth. Everyone who is of the truth hears My voice." - John 18:37

[Jesus] said to them, "Let us go somewhere else to the towns nearby, so that I may preach there also; for that is what I came for." - Mark 1:38

Do not think that I came to bring peace on the earth; I did not come to bring peace, but a sword. For I came to set a man against his father, and a daughter

against her mother, and a daughter-in-law against her mother-in-law.
- Matthew 10:34-35

I came that they may have life, and have it abundantly. - John 10:10

Jesus came to earth for the gospel. Each one of the above statements speaks directly about the gospel, or about Jesus teaching the gospel (Mark 1:38), or about the results of preaching the gospel (Matthew 10:34-35).

What is the gospel?

Paul provides a concise summary in his first letter to the Corinthians:

> *Now I make known to you, brethren, the gospel which I preached to you, which also you received, in which also you stand, by which also you are saved, if you hold fast the word which I preached to you, unless you believed in vain.*
>
> *For I delivered to you as of first importance what I also received, that Christ died for our sins according to the Scriptures, and that He was buried, and that He was raised on the third day according to the Scriptures...*
> - 1 Corinthians 15:1-4

How do we know this is true? First, because, as Paul says, it happened just as described in the scriptures. The prophecies in the Old Testament predicted Jesus' birth, life, death, and resurrection hundreds of years before Jesus was born. There are more than 300 prophecies about Jesus in the Old Testament. Every one of them was exactly and perfectly fulfilled.

And secondly, we know it is true because of all the eyewitnesses. As we continue reading in 1st Corinthians, Paul mentions there were hundreds of eyewitnesses, most of whom were still alive and could contradict Paul if anything he was writing was in error:

> *...and that He appeared to Cephas, then to the twelve. After that He appeared to more than five hundred brethren at one time, most of whom remain until now, but some have fallen asleep; then He appeared to James,*

then to all the apostles; and last of all, as to one untimely born, He appeared to me also. - 1 Corinthians 15-5-8

What is the cross about, and why did God have to go through all that pain and suffering?

The cross is a part of the gospel, a word that means "good news." Does that make sense? Jesus was beaten, tortured, and crucified on a cross... and that is good news? Yes, it is, but the good news is difficult to understand unless you know the bad news.

It's a fact that if you break the law, you must pay the penalty... unless, of course you don't get caught. When you are dealing with God, however, you are going to get caught. With God, you are not going to "get away with it." God is everywhere and He knows everything, even what you are thinking. You can't get away with anything. And you've done a lot of wrong things.

If we say, "We don't have any sin," we make Him [Jesus] *a liar*
— 1 John 1:10

To sin means to do things that God does not want you to do... in other words you've broken God's law. Jesus says you are a law-breaker. Are you going to call Jesus a liar?

Let's look at just a few of the Ten Commandments:

How many lies have you told? Have you ever taken something that does not belong to you? Have you ever looked with lust? In Matthew 5 Jesus says that looking with lust is the same as committing adultery in your heart. Have you ever done something in disobedience to your parents, or that dishonored your parents? Have you ever been angry at someone? Jesus said that if you are unrighteously angry with someone, you have murdered them in your heart. These are just five of the Ten Commandments. Did you answer "yes" to any of these questions?

Then you have broken God's laws.

For whoever keeps the entire law, yet fails in one point, is guilty of breaking it all. - James 2:10

That means you deserve God's just punishment... the eternal lake of fire. There is only one way to avoid it. Find someone, anyone who has lived a perfect life, who will die in your place.

That person is Jesus Christ.

2000 years ago Jesus lived a perfect life, then He died on the cross to pay the penalty you've earned for breaking God's laws. That's why Jesus came... that's why Jesus died on the cross.

Jesus promised that if you believed this... if you trust it is true... then Jesus gives Himself as a free gift to you. He gives you His death to pay your penalty for breaking God's laws. That means you are free from sin! You will join God in heaven!

And to demonstrate that His promise is true... that you can trust His promise... on the third day Jesus rose from the grave. He is alive, just as promised. And you can live also, by trusting in Jesus Christ as your savior from the penalty for sin.

This is the GOOD NEWS! This is the reason why Jesus came to the earth. This is the focus of the entire Bible. And this is what the cross is about and why it is such good news. But, this is not something *Jesus Calling* tells you. *Jesus Calling* is focused making you feel good. The real Jesus is focused on loving you and saving you.

But now Christ has been raised from the dead, the first fruits of those who are asleep. - 1 Corinthians 15:20

CHAPTER 28
TEST YOURSELF

Johnathan Edwards was probably the greatest American theologian. His preaching was the main tool God used in the First Great Awakening, with the revival beginning in Edward's church in Northampton, Massachusetts in the winter of 1734. He preached in that church for 22 years and was famous for his sermon *"Sinners in the Hands of an Angry God."* But in 1749, after 22 years, by a vote of 200 to 23 his congregation voted him out.

Why?

Because he would not allow people to take communion unless they confessed Jesus Christ as their Lord and savior. Scripture is clear (1 Corinthians 11), but it appears that a majority of this great preacher's congregation were not believers.

Not everyone who thinks they are a Christian, is truly a Christian. Jesus gives a dire warning in the Sermon on the Mount:

"Not everyone who says to Me, 'Lord, Lord,' will enter the kingdom of heaven, but he who does the will of My Father who is in heaven will enter. Many will say to Me on that day, 'Lord, Lord, did we not prophesy in Your name, and in Your name cast out demons, and in Your name perform many miracles?' And then I will declare to them, 'I never knew you; DEPART FROM ME, YOU WHO PRACTICE LAWLESSNESS.' - Matthew 7:21-23

What is this saying?

There are people who think they are going to heaven, and they are not. In fact, according to Jesus, there are "many" people who think they know Jesus and are saved, but they have been deceiving themselves.

Even people who seem very religious, always speaking with religious words and calling Jesus "Lord, Lord," are not necessarily saved. While using foul language can be a sign you are not saved, using a lot of Christian words and phrases, so that you sound very "holy," is not a sign that you are a saved Christian.

Even people who appear to be so close to Jesus that they prophesy in the name of Jesus... even people who cast out demons... even people who have performed many miracles in the name of Jesus... surely these people are be saved. But, Jesus says "I never knew you. Depart from me you who practice lawlessness." None of these are signs that a person is saved.

Surely our Christian leaders who serve Christ every day, and who look so good, and who speak using many religious words, and who even have done many good works and amazing miracles... surely these people are heading for heaven. But, Jesus says, *"I never knew you; DEPART FROM ME, YOU WHO PRACTICE LAWLESSNESS."*

The point Jesus is making is that neither your outward appearances, nor your religious words and actions, nor your good works demonstrate salvation. In Matthew 24:24 Jesus makes the point that there will be false saviors and false prophets... and even people who will do false miracles:

> *"False messiahs and false prophets will arise and perform great signs and wonders to lead astray, if possible, even the elect."* - Matthew 24:24

These "religious" people will appear to be very good. They will appear to be from God and be of God. They will even believe they are from God and that they are doing God's work. But they are not.

Jesus is giving examples of the extreme. People who are involved in ministry, and who appear to be very Christian and very close to God. But, appearances can be deceiving. It's not looks and outward actions that are important, it's what is in your heart. People can appear very religious, but not be truly saved.

And this applies to us ordinary people also.

Vast numbers of ordinary people think they are Christians and are confident they are going to heaven, but they are not. In Matthew chapter 7 Jesus talks about the wide gate. It is the gate to hell through which masses of people, many believing they are Christians, are passing through. They will all hear Jesus say, *"Sorry I never knew you."* These are words you never want to hear from Jesus.

So, what are we to do? Scripture never presents a problem without giving the solution. The solution is to test yourself to see if you are in the faith.

> *Test yourselves to see if you are in the faith. Examine yourselves. Or do you yourselves not recognize that Jesus Christ is in you?—unless you fail the test. And I hope you will recognize that we do not fail the test.* – 2 Corinthians 13:5-6

How do we test ourselves? What criteria do we use? Scripture answers those questions also. For example 1st John gives ten tests to see if you are in the faith. These include:

- Do you enjoy spending time with Christians? And do you actually spend time with other Christians? (The correct answer is yes.)

- Do you practice sin or do you strive to obey God? Over the years have you seen a growing distaste for sin in yourself, and an increasing love of righteousness? (The correct answers are: I strive to obey God and yes, I have a growing distaste for sin.)

- Are you reading your Bible daily? (The correct answer is yes.)

- Do you hate any of your Christian brothers or sisters? (The correct answer is no.) If you have a dispute with a Christian brother or sister, do you get it resolved quickly, without resorting to the courts? (The correct answer is yes.)

- Do you regularly confess your sins to God? (The correct answer is yes.)

These are not mechanical things you do because they are on a "to-do" list. These are things Christians desire to do. A perfect score is not required. What is important is that you see a trend of growing more in conformance with these "tests." Also look to be growing in conformance with the Beatitudes (see previous chapters) during your Christian life.

A key indicator that someone is saved is that they experience a growing knowledge of sin, and an increasing desire to turn away from sin. Another way to say this is that you are experiencing a growing knowledge of the will of God, and an increasing desire to obey God in all things. For example:

- As I talked about in chapter 18, do you mourn over sin? *Blessed are those who mourn* [over sin], *for they shall be comforted.* – Matthew 5:4

- Do you run from sin? *Run from sexual immorality!* - 1 Corinthians 6:18

- When you sin, do you confess that sin to God? God has promised that if you confess your sin, you will be forgiven. *If we confess our sins, He is faithful and righteous to forgive us our sins and to cleanse us from all unrighteousness.* - 1 John 1:9

- Are there thoughts and behaviors that were acceptable several years ago, and today you find them so sinful that they are unthinkable? If so, you are growing to be more like Christ.

- Finally, and think carefully about this one, are you the same inside as you are on the outside? Do you truly desire what is pure and righteous? Do you have a strong desire to know and understand scripture? Are you continually striving to change the way you think and act? Or do you put on a show, appearing good on the outside, but holding anger, hate, or lust inside?

That's what the Pharisees in the time of Jesus were like. Clean and good looking on the outside, and dead inside.

Woe to you, scribes and Pharisees, hypocrites! For you are like whitewashed tombs which on the outside appear beautiful, but inside they are full of dead men's bones and all uncleanness. So you, too, outwardly appear righteous to men, but inwardly you are full of hypocrisy and lawlessness. – Matthew 23:27-28

Examine yourself, and if you find yourself falling short, turn to Jesus Christ. Repent, confessing your sins to God, and trust that Jesus Christ has paid your penalty for sin in full.

These are facts you'll never hear about in books like *Jesus Calling*. Books that lead you to feel good, but are leading you away from the truth you need.

You've read the true words of Jesus in this book. His #1 concern is that you be saved. He loves you, and more than anything He wants you to turn from your sin and walk in obedience to God. Will you do that? Will you commit today to following the true Jesus of the Bible? Our prayers are with you.

More information about testing yourself is available on our church web site at: http://tiny.cc/wqkt4x

CHAPTER 29
IF *JESUS CALLING* IS NOT CHRISTIAN, WHAT IS IT?

I hope this book has thoroughly demonstrated that Jesus Calling is not a Christian book. What we have in *Jesus Calling* is a book filled with teaching that is not in agreement with scripture, we have a false gospel, and a "Jesus" that is not the Jesus of the Bible

So, what is Jesus Calling?

An excellent book called *"Another Jesus Calling"* by Warren B. Smith answers that question. Mr. Smith is a Christian who came out of the New Age movement. He has an in-depth knowledge and understanding of New Age teaching and principles. Here's what he says in the introduction to his book:

"Having been formerly involved in the New Age movement, I became immediately concerned when I read the book [Jesus Calling]. It was troubling for me to see a number of New Age practices and concepts being presented as completely normal for Christians. Even more troubling, there were no warnings or disclaimers about what was being introduced. By the end of the book, Jesus Calling and its "Jesus" had subtly and not so subtly introduced occult/New Age channeling, spiritual dictation, creative visualization, meditation, divine alchemy, co-creation with God, and practicing the presence like it was everyday Christian fare. New Age terms and concepts were brought into the messages like they were no big deal. And added to this were indirect references to a pantheistic poet and two classic

New Age books, along with a hearty endorsement of God Calling—the channeled book that inspired Sarah Young to try and receive her own personal messages from Jesus."

"The unusual use of language by the "Jesus" of Jesus Calling was also disturbing. It seemed to run the gamut from "everyday Joe" language to strange word choice, unwarranted flattery, worldly clichés, repetitive phrases, disparaging comments, and not-so-subtle mockery. All in all, Jesus Calling seemed to be an obvious attempt by our spiritual Adversary to get an even further foothold inside the Christian church." - Warren B. Smith, Another Jesus Calling, 2013, pages 12 & 13.

Jesus Calling is not a Christian book. Warren Smith gets it exactly right. *Jesus Calling* is packed with New Age teaching disguised using Christian phraseology.

If you get the chance, I recommend reading Warren Smith's book, *"Another Jesus Calling"* to learn more about what Jesus Calling really is about. Visit: http://www.warrenbsmith.com

CHAPTER 30
MY THOUGHTS ONLY

I hope you have found the information in this book to be useful. What is in this book are my fallible thoughts and opinions on the *Jesus Calling* devotional book. I do not claim to have any inspiration or leading from the Holy Spirit. So if there are errors, they are mine. If I have misrepresented God in any way, the fault is mine.

I have done my best to be accurate and true to the truth of scripture. I have immersed myself in scripture and continue to do so. I have taken advantage of the best resources I have available to help me understand scripture. I have been in prayer asking the Lord to help me ensure this book is true and accurate, but that does not mean that my will has never inadvertently imposed itself, possibly even in opposition to God's desires. I am a wretched sinner who falls far short of God's standards.

I have not received messages from God concerning this book, nor any discernable leading of the Spirit. I claim no special relationship with Jesus, other than that of His being my Lord and Savior.

I hope and pray that He is also your Lord and Savior. That is the only way to be in the presence of Jesus.

ABOUT THE AUTHOR

Steve Hudgik served as the pastor of the Cannon Beach Bible Church, in Cannon Beach, Oregon from 2013 until September 2018, and then as an associate pastor until October 2019.

Steve has been the executive director of the Move to Assurance (MTA) ministry since 2000. MTA is involved in evangelism, outreach, and apologetics ministries. Some of the MTA web sites include:

www.911Christ.com
www.MTAbible.com
www.MoveToAssurance.org
www.SciencePastor.com
www.DinosaursForJesus.com

**Other books by Steve Hudgik
are available on Amazon.com**

OTHER CHRISTIAN BOOKS
BY STEVE HUDGIK

Did God Really Say?
Answering humanist attacks on the bible.
Steve goes to the American Humanist web site and
answers every accusation and attack they make against scripture and
the Bible.

Mrs. Bartlett and Her Class
at the Metropolitan Tabernacle
Written by her son Edward (with notes and annotations by Steve),
this is the amazing true story about a prayer warrior and evangelist in
Charles Spurgeon's church.

The Presence of God
A commentary on the book of Esther
Esther is the only book in the bible that does not mention God, yet
God's presence can be seen throughout this book

Sarah Young's Jesus Always Devotional EXPOSED!
Shining the light of scripture on the unbiblical
teaching of the *Jesus Always* devotional.

Happy Are The...
Discovering joy through the beatitudes

All of Steve's books are available on Amazon

Made in the USA
Monee, IL
21 April 2022

95127041R00089